Assassins

Gabriel Khan is the pseudonym for a veteran crime reporter from Mumbai. With experience of over twenty-five years in journalism—mainly print and stints with television and dotcoms—Gabriel is a reservoir of information on the city's underbelly. Gabriel has also done a lot of handholding for several budding journalists, many of whom have now established their bylines.

After making his debut with *Special 26* (the story of Neeraj Pandey's eponymous thriller), Gabriel Khan co-authored with S. Hussain Zaidi on his debut fiction, *Mumbai Avengers*, which was subsequently made into a blockbuster movie titled *Phantom*, directed by Kabir Khan.

This is Gabriel Khan's third book based on real-life incidents.

ASSASINS

GABRIEL
KHAN

First published by Westland Publications Private Limited in 2020

1st Floor, A Block, East Wing, Plot No. 40, SP Infocity, Dr MGR Salai, Perungudi, Kandanchavadi, Chennai 600096

Westland and the Westland logo are the trademarks of Westland Publications Private Limited, or its affiliates.

ISBN: 9789389648195

10 9 8 7 6 5 4 3 2 1

This is a work of fiction. Names, characters, organisations, places, events and incidents are either products of the author's imagination or used fictitiously.

Typeset by SÜRYA, New Delhi
Printed at Manipal Technologies Limited, Manipal

For
My real-life
Venus

1

THE MAN WAS becoming decidedly more annoying, but she had dealt with worse. Much worse.

So, as he once again tried to strike up a conversation, she simply pulled out a book from her bag, opened it, and started reading.

'Oho! Shayari! I love shayari!' the man said, looking at the title of her book. 'It touches something deep inside me. So stirring! Urdu is such a beautiful language!'

Coolly, she shut the book and turned to him.

'You like poetry?' she asked.

'Oh, I love it!'

'Who is your favourite poet?' she asked.

'Oh ... oh ...' he stuttered. 'I don't have a favourite poet as such. I focus more on the content, not the writer.'

'Your favourite poem then,' she asked, giving him a smile.

The smile encouraged him and his chest puffed up.

'Koi deewana kehta hai, koi pagal samajhta hai;
Magar dharti ki bechaini ko bas baadal samajhta hai!'

She inwardly shook her head. The man was quoting a verse by Dr Kumar Vishwas, which every lovelorn teenager had adopted as their anthem.

'Your turn,' he said, confident that he had successfully caught her interest. 'What's your favourite poem?'

'Oh, you know ...' she said, playing with her hair.

'Come on, I'd love to hear it,' he said.

'Ishrat-e-qatra hai dariya mein fanaa ho jaana;
Dard ka hadh se guzarna hai dawaa ho jaana.'

The verse by Mirza Ghalib had the desired effect. He stared at her uncomprehendingly, his mouth half-open for a few seconds before he pulled out his cell phone and muttered something unintelligible.

Smiling sweetly at him, she slid the book inside her bag, slung it over her shoulder and walked towards the boarding gate. The sign for boarding had just been turned on. *None too soon*, she thought to herself.

As the line for boarding moved, she glanced idly at the TV screen in the lobby and caught sight of a familiar face. A news channel was running an 'exclusive' interview with 'underworld don' Shakti Pillai. He had called the channel's office earlier in the day, and they were running the conversation.

Don believed to be in the Middle East—the ticker read.

She chuckled. He wasn't in the Middle East. He was in Bangkok. Where she was going.

Her passport identified her as Saba Mansoor, aged thirty-five, resident of New Delhi. And her visiting cards claimed she was a photographer. Very few people knew who she really was. For a fleeting moment, she almost felt like revealing the scars left behind by three bullet wounds under her left breast to the annoying man in the lobby, just to see the look on his face. But then, she thought, she would have to kill him.

Saba's journey to Bangkok had its roots in the bitter fury of one of Mumbai's top industrialists who had sworn revenge against Shakti Pillai, whatever the cost.

The industrialist, Amarchand Mehra, had been the happiest man in the world six weeks ago, having fixed his daughter's marriage to the son of his childhood friend and media magnate Amitabh Bose. The wedding was announced with much fanfare and Mehra's phone hadn't stopped ringing ever since. Everybody who was anybody was calling to express their good wishes so that they could be invited to the lavish wedding and get the chance to be captured in the same frame as Mehra and Bose.

So it was without much thought that he answered a call from an unknown number three days after the announcement. The caller turned out to be Shakti Pillai.

'You are spending quite a lot of cash these days, Mehra,' he began. 'Send some of it my way too.'

'Who is this?' Mehra asked, annoyed.

'This is Shakti Pillai,' the gangster replied, 'and if you are smart, you will have ten crore in cash ready in a week.'

'Are you threatening me, you two-bit piece of shit?' Mehra asked furiously.

'Calling me names is not going to change the facts, Mehra. And the facts are that if you don't pay this little donation, you will have to cancel that much hyped wedding.'

Pillai ended the call before Mehra could go on. Mehra speed-dialled the police commissioner who, after spending ten minutes calming Mehra down, assured him that Pillai would not touch a hair on his head.

'The zonal DCP will personally be enforcing security at your daughter's wedding. You have my word on that,' the top cop assured Mehra.

Exactly one week later, Pillai called again.

Mehra listened to him identify himself before saying, 'I don't know if you have a hearing problem or something, but you remain a two-bit piece of shit in my eyes.'

After a few seconds of silence, Pillai said, 'You are responsible for what I am about to do,' and hung up.

Mehra called the police commissioner again, and he doubled his and his family's security within the hour.

Roughly six hours later, Mehra's phone rang again. He was poring over some files in his study at his Nepean Sea Road house and absently answered the call without checking the caller ID.

'You know,' Pillai said on the other end, 'you should really teach your daughter some basic cybersecurity.'

Mehra felt a cold hand wrap itself around his heart. Whatever he had been expecting, the word 'cybersecurity' hadn't figured in it.

'What the fuck ...' was all he could manage.

'Check your email,' Pillai said before the line went dead.

Mehra hastily logged into his email, fumbling over the keys twice before getting it right. The latest email contained a link to a social media page. He clicked on the link and felt himself freeze.

Someone had created a Facebook page dedicated to his daughter, and it was full of pictures of herself in the shower and in her bedroom in various stages of undress. There were also some pictures of her with some female friends, topless, in a private villa in Bali, where she had gone on a trip last year. Her friends had been blurred out, and only she could be seen clearly. Another picture showed his daughter sprawled sideways across the laps of three young men roughly her age at what appeared to be a house party.

Mehra willed himself to move, scrolling downwards, making himself look at all the pictures. Just as he was done, his personal assistant came running into the study, sweating and trembling. For a long moment, both men started at each other's faces. Then the PA spoke.

'Some ... some pictures ... have gone viral ... on WhatsApp ...'

'RASHMI!' Mehra roared as he sprang out of his chair and stormed to his daughter's room. 'Rashmi!' he shouted as he reached her door. It was ajar. He kicked it open and stomped inside, coming to a halt at her bed. Rashmi was sitting on the bed, crying uncontrollably. Her phone was lying on her lap.

With shaking hands, he picked up the phone and saw that she had been looking at the same Facebook page. Mehra flung the phone aside and kicked the bed hard before going to the window, breathing heavily.

Two days later, Bose and his entire family visited the Mehra residence. That same evening, the wedding was officially called off, citing 'personal reasons'.

Of course, everyone knew the reasons, including the news media, who camped outside Mehra's house for a week before losing interest. Rashmi's friends started an online campaign of sorts, and within half a day enough people had reported the page to Facebook. The head of the Cyber Crime cell of the Mumbai Police visited him to tell him that they were trying to trace the IP address. The commissioner of police called several times to convince him to register a formal complaint against Pillai. Mehra only responded with stoic silence.

In the privacy of his study, Mehra studied each and every news item concerning Shakti Pillai and jotted down details about his modus operandi. Through his trusty PA, he gathered information about every businessman, small or powerful, who had ever been attacked, in any way, by the gangster. He invited the Crime Branch cops for a quiet drink at his house and wheedled out whatever he could about the fugitive, including his location. Of course, the cops knew where he was, no matter what they told the media. After a lot of cajoling and bribing, Mehra finally received confirmation that Pillai was in Bangkok.

And after completing his research, he invited seven industrialists as rich and powerful as him to his holiday home in Seychelles for a discreet conference.

'I guess you all know by now why we're here,' Mehra began.

'Shakti Pillai,' said one businessman.

'Son of a bitch,' said another.

'Yes,' Mehra said. 'But a clever one.'

Without waiting for anyone to speak, Mehra went on.

'This is a new breed of criminal, gentlemen. He is desperate to make a name in a world that has been ruled by very few till now. He is young, hungry and, above all, he is clever. He thinks outside the box. Instead of the usual armed men shooting at our storefronts to force money out of us, he is actually using modern methods to his advantage.'

There were nods and murmurs around the room.

Mehra turned to the man sitting on his left.

'He hired Mumbai-based private detectives to follow you,' Mehra said. 'Got pictures of you with your mistress and sent them to your wife. How much are you paying her in alimony now?'

'Too bloody much,' the businessman growled.

Mehra turned to another man.

'He hacked into your email and sent the plans of your latest product to your competitor. How much did you lose when they launched the same product before you did?'

'A hundred and fifty fucking crores,' the man spat out.

Mehra nodded.

'That's why he is dangerous. He is no longer threatening to kill us. He is threatening to destroy us. My daughter has been on suicide watch for the last four weeks. And the bastard's made sure everyone knows it was him. The next man he calls won't think twice before paying up whatever he demands.'

'Did he hire you to be his PR agent or something, Mehra? Is that why we're here?' one of them asked.

Mehra shook his head.

'We're here so that we can put a stop to him while we still can,' he announced. 'And by stop, I mean kill.'

There was silence for almost a minute before the room erupted. For the next three hours, Mehra argued that putting Pillai down was really the best thing to do. One by one, he convinced them all. It was not easy. These men were sharks, but of a different kind. The only stabbing they did was figurative. A couple of men in the room could not even stand the sight of blood. They were ruthless, but they lived in a different world.

Finally, the men settled down.

'How?' one of them asked.

There was a polite cough at the far end of the room, as Dilshad Rehman, one of the city's top security solutions providers, stood up.

'I have a friend,' he said. 'Someone I knew back in the army, who is now in the arms business. He … knows people we can hire.'

'Is it safe? For us, I mean?'

Khan nodded. 'Give me a few days. Shall we meet again in, say, a week?' he said.

And so it was that one week later, each of the eight men who had gathered in Seychelles met again, this time in Barcelona.

Rehman handed Mehra a folder.

'Contact numbers, email IDs, bank accounts. The assassin ...' Everyone except Khan and Mehra flinched at the word. ' ... prefers to be called by the name Venus. She—'

'It's a *woman*?' one of them said.

Khan ignored the interruption. He had seen too much patriarchy and misogyny in his own house to waste time arguing about it. 'She has asked us to avoid phone calls unless absolutely important and would prefer to converse via email.'

'Anything else?' Mehra asked.

'She needs a final price by tonight.'

After much haggling—they were businessmen after all—the eight men agreed to pool in a hundred crore rupees each. It was decided that the money would be transferred to a single account the same day. The account would be operated by Mehra and Khan, and they would provide spending money to Venus as per her requirements, and pay the balance when the job was done. The option of a bonus at the end of the operation was kept open.

And so, a week later, Venus, bearing an Indian passport identifying her as Saba Mansoor, was going over the plan in her mind one more time before boarding her flight to Bangkok.

2

POLICE COMMISSIONER SANJAY MATHUR was excited and nervous at the same time.

An Indian Police Service officer of the encounter era, Mathur had personally shot down two gangsters as a deputy commissioner with the Mumbai Crime Branch. Later, when he returned to the Crime Branch as joint commissioner, he picked out the best officers the force had to offer and gave them a free hand as long as they did not get into trouble. Scores of gangsters were killed in encounters sanctioned by him till the bad press got too much and orders came from the higher-ups to stop.

Mathur was a firm believer in the encounter school of thought: If you know they are guilty, kill them and move on. Which was why Shakti Pillai was a huge thorn in his side.

The episode with Mehra was only the latest in a string of failures when it came to Pillai. Every time Mathur was approached by some big figure or another from Mumbai, seeking protection from Pillai, he would promise them that the Mumbai Police would do everything it could. And every time, Pillai, sitting in

Bangkok, would do something like hack into an email account or hire a private eye, causing losses to the tune of crores to his targets. Other times, he would simply launch brazen shootings in broad daylight and claim responsibility an hour later by calling the news media.

The Crime Branch officers informed Mathur that Pillai was successfully striking terror in people, and they were no longer approaching the police, opting instead to pay whatever Pillai demanded.

After Mehra's daughter's pictures went viral, Mathur tried to convince Mehra to register a complaint. The first time Mathur called, Mehra listened calmly and then hung up without saying a word. The next time, Mehra simply refused to take his call.

Time and again, Mathur had found himself wishing that Pillai were in Mumbai, or anywhere in India, so that he could just finish off the bastard once and for all.

It was only the previous night, while watching the news with a glass of wine by his side, that the germ of an idea spawned in his head. The chief of the Metropolitan Police, who was responsible for law and order in Bangkok and its suburbs, was giving an interview to an international channel about the state of crime in his city. Mathur didn't even realise it till it began taking shape, and when it did, he straightened up and sniffed his glass to make sure it was indeed wine he was drinking.

The entire night Mathur turned the plan over and over in his head, letting it grow and develop till it had taken form and was staring him in the face. The next morning he made a call from his personal cell phone to Narong Anantasu, the commissioner of the Metropolitan Police, in Bangkok. Both men knew each other, having met at a global conference on terror eleven years ago, and had stayed in touch. And more importantly, Anantasu owed Mathur a favour.

In 2010, a British woman had been found murdered in a five-star hotel in Bangkok. She had checked into the hotel three days before the murder, and the only visitor she'd had was a man who was later identified as Sumit Chandra, an Indian national who had befriended the woman when she was on a trip to India. The woman, Olivia Hall, had undergone a bitter divorce, and Chandra, who was rich, good-looking and charming, had wooed her till she had fallen madly in love with him. She had wanted to marry Chandra, but there was a problem: he had no intention of committing to her and was already on the hunt for his next girlfriend.

Olivia began calling Chandra fifty times a day and even turned up at his workplace, after which he convinced her to leave the country and wait for him in Bangkok, telling her that his parents were opposed to the marriage and that they could elope when he came to Bangkok for a business meeting. Chandra joined her in Bangkok, spent the night with her in her hotel room, slit her throat when she was asleep, and was on a flight to India before the body was discovered.

When Mathur and Anantasu met for the first time at the global conference, Mathur was joint commissioner,

Crime Branch. Anantasu took the opportunity to gripe about the fact that the Mumbai Police had done nothing to try and trace Chandra, who the Bangkok Police knew was in India. Mathur just nodded indulgently and made a mental note of it.

After returning to India, Mathur called some of his best officers and promised a glowing positive remark in the Annual Confidential Report for the first officer to give him a confirmed report on Chandra's whereabouts. Two weeks later, an enterprising police inspector with Unit III called him.

'Sir, Chandra is in Nanded. He sends money to his mother in Mumbai every month and I traced his account details. He's married now and has a son,' the officer said, followed by the customary question every cop asked in such a scenario. 'Shall we pick him up, sir?'

To his great disappointment, Mathur replied, 'Get there and watch him, but do nothing.'

Mathur then called Anantasu.

Within twelve hours, a team of officers from the Metropolitan Police landed in India and Chandra was arrested jointly by the Metropolitan and the Mumbai Police. He was taken to Bangkok with much fanfare and Anantasu was hailed as a hero in the Thai, as well as the British press.

'Mathur, my friend,' Anantasu told the Mumbai cop. 'If you ever need my help, for any damn thing, all you have to do is tell me.'

That morning, Mathur called in the favour before leaving for work. Now, as he paced about his office, he was aware of a sheen of sweat on his forehead. If this worked, it would be the biggest thing he ever pulled off. If it didn't ... well, he didn't want to think about that possibility.

There was a discreet knock on the door and his orderly entered.

'Agarkar,' the orderly said politely. Mathur nodded and sat down at his desk. The orderly withdrew, and a few seconds later, a tall, hefty man entered, walked up to Mathur's desk, saluted smartly and stood at attention.

Mathur contemplated his subordinate silently for a few seconds. Police Inspector Dayanand Agarkar had recently been reinstated to the Mumbai Police, having been cleared after the last of the departmental inquiries against him. A former encounter specialist, Agarkar had killed a string of notorious gangsters under Mathur's leadership before his dismissal over charges of corruption. After three years of investigation, the charges against him were dropped and Agarkar approached the Maharashtra Administrative Tribunal seeking reinstatement. After another year of hearings, the tribunal ruled in his favour and Agarkar returned to his former rank.

Mathur didn't care if the charges against Agarkar were true. All he knew about Agarkar was that the man was able to follow orders, and was of the same school of thought as he was when it came to killing criminals.

'Sit, Agarkar,' Mathur said.

The junior cop thanked his boss and took a chair.

'Good work on the drug bust.'

'Thank you, sir.' Agarkar beamed.

After his reinstatement, Agarkar, who had thrived on bumping off gangland elements, found himself at sea for a short while. This was a new world for him, where guns were rarely fired and the term 'human rights' actually meant something. But, like Mathur had known he would, Agarkar quickly adapted to the situation. He identified the latest 'in thing' when it came to crime—mephedrone. The drug was the latest rage, due to a variety of reasons. It gave the user a high, it helped them lose weight and it enhanced sexual performance. By the time the police woke up to the threat and the government included it in the Narcotics Drugs and Psychotropic Substances Act, half the city had become addicted to it.

Agarkar, who was posted with the Andheri police, squeezed every drug dealer in his jurisdiction till he hit pay dirt. One of them finally told him where the drugs were coming from, and a week later, a team from Andheri Police Station, led by Police Inspector Agarkar, raided a lab in Palghar that was producing mephedrone by the ton every night after the nearby villages went to sleep. Agarkar was a hero again.

Now, as he sat glowing in front of Mathur, the top cop congratulated himself on his choice. He had picked the right man for the job.

'How much do you know about Shakti Pillai?' Mathur asked.

Agarkar's face changed.

'Needs to be dealt with before he gets out of hand, sir. We took him lightly for too long.'

Mathur nodded approvingly. Picking up his phone, he asked his orderly to get tea for them before continuing.

'He's in Bangkok these days. Moved there soon after his split from Maqsood Alam,' he said.

Agarkar nodded. 'I'm told he's got his fingers in a lot of pies there and keeps the local cops very happy.'

'While in India, he's getting bigger by the day,' Mathur growled. 'Apart from those hit jobs he keeps taking for any and every one, he's into cybercrime now. I'm hearing about him hiring hackers to develop viruses, and frankly, that is bloody scary.'

'If he'd been in Mumbai, I would've taken him out by now, sir,' Agarkar said.

He knew he could speak freely in Mathur's presence because they'd had innumerable conversations such as this back when they were both in the Crime Branch. The solution that both the cops were thinking of, if Pillai were in Mumbai, was simple: pick him up, take him to a suitable spot, kill him and plant a couple of guns on his body, after which they would tell the media that he had tried to attack them and that they were forced to return fire.

'How would you like to do that?' Mathur said.

Agarkar stared uncomprehendingly. Mathur didn't blame the poor man.

'How would you like to kill Pillai?' Mathur said.

Agarkar nearly fell off his chair but checked himself as Mathur's orderly entered with a teapot and cups on a tray.

Mathur made tea for them while watching Agarkar chew on what he had just said, struggling to come up with a suitable response.

'In ... in Bangkok, sir?' Agarkar asked finally.

Mathur nodded.

'An encounter ... on ... on foreign soil?' Agarkar was still trying to wrap his head around the idea.

'Don't be silly.' Mathur smiled. 'That would be a criminal offence.'

Agarkar finally gave up and waited for his superior to explain.

'I have a friend in the Royal Thai Police,' Mathur began, leaning forward in his chair. 'He has agreed to help me out, but I need someone I can trust, and someone who will get the job done.'

Agarkar felt his chest puff up a little.

'We know he's in Bangkok, and we know he's running several rackets there. He has somehow managed to keep a layer between himself and these operations, not to mention bribing the local police well enough to be able to learn when they are coming for him.'

Agarkar nodded.

'Which is why we need someone who is not on his payroll. The Bangkok Police chief has agreed to help you out in every way he can, if you help him in return.'

'And how do I do that, sir?'

'You knew Pillai back when he was here, before he fled to Bangkok. And you know who his close aides are. Very few of our current lot have the kind of knowledge you do. Share this information with the Bangkok Police chief. He's putting together a small team of trusted men. Work with them. Find Pillai's inner circle. Get to Pillai,' Mathur said.

'And the Thai government will agree to extradition, sir?' Agarkar asked.

Mathur smiled.

'Who said anything about extradition?'

Agarkar, who had picked up his cup to take a sip, felt his hand tremble a little.

'That's right,' Mathur said, still smiling. 'Shoot the bastard. Plant a gun or two on his body. The usual, right?'

Agarkar put his cup down.

'Will our government—'

'Fuck our government,' Mathur snapped. 'Once Pillai is dead and they find out we were involved, they'll fall over themselves to claim a share of the credit. And by default, they will have to give you some as well.'

Agakar nodded slowly, finally getting Mathur's drift.

'So, till it actually happens ...'

Mathur nodded.

'Till Pillai is actually dead, this will have to be top secret. Nobody except you and me can know about this. And I mean nobody. Officially, you're going on a holiday. Apply for leave today and leave the rest to me.'

Agarkar nodded.

'Just one thing,' Mathur said, rising from his seat and walking around his desk to where Agarkar was sitting.

'You will have to let the Bangkok Police claim the credit for the actual encounter. But you will come back as the officer who made it all possible,' he said.

'And if something goes wrong?'

'I will claim ignorance, officially.'

Agarkar sipped his tea silently.

'What do you say?' Mathur asked. 'Karega?'

Agarkar smiled.

'Karoonga, sir.'

3

It was 1.20 a.m. in Mumbai when Venus saw Shakti Pillai's interview on the news channel, while waiting to board her flight to Bangkok. Due to the one-and-a-half hour time difference, it was 11.50 p.m. the previous day in Dubai when Maqsood Alam saw the same interview in his suite at the Burj Khalifa hotel, while sipping Scotch on the rocks.

As he readjusted his bulky frame in the comfortable chair, Alam let his mind wander.

Alam had been all of sixteen years old when he had committed his first murder as part of a turf war in Dongri, where he had been born. The son of a peon with what was then called the Bombay Municipal Corporation, Alam started dreaming big at a very young age. And his dreams included lavish bungalows and coffers filled with gold, which his father, a very unambitious man, could not provide. Alam took to stealing whatever he wanted, and as he grew up, he fell into the company of local young thugs, who taught him that there was no need to steal when you could take things by force.

The murder, which Alam committed during a clash between his group and one from the lane adjacent theirs, changed him in more ways than one and set him on a path that eventually led him to the plush room at the Burj Khalifa.

After killing the rival gang member, Alam went home and told his father what he had done. His father's first reaction was to thrash the living daylights out of him. After he had calmed down, he took Alam to meet the local mafia don, Amjad Fareed Rehman, who had earned the name Haji Baba after his pilgrimage to Haj several years ago.

Haji Baba stroked his dense white beard thoughtfully as he listened to Alam's father and then sent for the parents of the boy that Alam had killed. In clipped tones, Haji Baba told the dead boy's parents that Alam was remorseful for what he had done—Alam had the good sense to keep his mouth shut—and that Alam's family was prepared to compensate them.

'True, nothing can make up for the loss of a loved one,' Haji Baba said. 'But don't forget that God forgives even those who ask for penance with an honest heart. It is up to you to be large-hearted and put a stop to this violence instead of letting it multiply. For this, they will pay you every penny they have saved up. And you will be doing me a favour by not bringing the police into my mohalla. In future, if you ever find yourself in need of anything, all you have to do is ask.'

Alam watched in awe as Haji Baba settled the matter without uttering a single threat or raising a single weapon. He realised that the don could only do this because he had the one thing no one else, at least in the locality, had. Power.

The next day, Alam dropped out of school and went to work for Haji Baba.

'I want to repay you for what you have done for me,' a deceptively polite Alam told the don, who only smiled and patted the young man's shoulder.

For the next ten years, Alam steadily worked his way up the ladder in Haji Baba's gang, all the time observing and assimilating as much as he could. He had understood the benefits of power, and now he was learning how to acquire it. Within a year of working for Haji Baba, Alam was doing small favours for kids his age who lived in his lane. A dispute settled here, a piece of information obtained there, a meeting set up elsewhere: all of it added to Alam's image as a man who could get things done, and soon, people from all over his basti started approaching him for favours.

Apart from this growing reputation, Alam also had the badge of honour of working under Haji Baba, a badge that he intended to exploit to the fullest. People seeking audience with Haji Baba started requesting Alam to put in a word. Aware of the power he wielded, Alam listened to each one carefully before rejecting them, till he found the most suitable candidate: a neighbour whose teenage daughter had become pregnant after falling prey to the charms of the local Casanova. The girl's father had all but begged the boy to marry her to keep his name from becoming mud in the locality. The playboy, an eighteen-year-old named Sagir, had only laughed in the old man's face.

That night, after Haji Baba had finished his dinner and was chewing a paan, Alam softly asked him, 'Baba, what is your position on violence?'

Haji Baba looked up at Alam, who was now eighteen, and said, 'I tend to avoid it, but that is not always possible. Why do you ask, beta?'

In a polite tone, Alam narrated the plight of the pregnant girl and her father, and ended by saying, 'Baba, I have made inquiries. This is not the first girl that this boy has exploited in such a manner. I know that one word from you and he will agree to marry the girl. But what guarantee do we have that he will not take advantage of other girls even after getting married? Does it not, in such a case, become necessary to use more extreme methods?'

Haji Baba looked at Alam for a long moment, during which time Alam waited with his heart pounding in his chest. Finally, Haji Baba smiled slightly.

'You are growing up, beta,' he said. After a pause, he added, 'Do what you think is right. I'd like to see your judgement.'

The next evening, Alam gathered four of his friends, the same ones with whom he had committed his first murder, and went looking for Sagir. They found him at the local barber's shop, lounging about on one of the chairs, carefully running a comb through his thick hair.

'Salaam, Maqsood bhai!' Sagir greeted cheerily as Alam entered the barbershop. 'Feel like a shave? Our

Farookh bhai here will have you looking like a movie star in no time,' Sagir said, gesturing towards the barber who, having sensed trouble, was already edging towards the door.

'Farhana,' was all Alam said.

Sagir's smile slipped a little.

'Who?' he asked.

Casually, Alam picked up one of the barber's razors from the dressing table and slowly opened it.

'Raheem chacha's daughter, Farhana, who is pregnant, thanks to you. I have come to ask you if you will marry her. But hear this, Sagir, I will only ask you once,' Alam said, dangerously calm as he inserted a fresh blade into the razor.

Sagir slowly stood up from the barber's chair and Alam turned around to face him.

'Maqsood,' Sagir said. 'I know your reputation and I know who you work for. But bear in mind that my father is the local corporator's right-hand man.'

'Is that a no?' Alam asked.

'Yes, you cheap hooligan. That is a no,' Sagir snarled. It was the last thing he did with his face without wincing for the next several weeks.

Without warning, Alam brought the razor up in one swift movement and flicked it across Sagir's face. The latter's hand shot up reflexively and was quickly drenched in his own blood, which was flowing freely from the long gash that Alam had made across his cheek. Before Sagir could react, Alam kicked him in the gut, and when he doubled over, he dragged him by his hair out of the shop and into the street.

Over the next ten minutes, Sagir was punched and kicked around while people gathered. As the crowd began to swell, two of Alam's friends whipped out daggers and kept the people at bay. The other two held Sagir while Alam, still clutching the razor, proceeded to inflict cut after cut on the Casanova's face. All the while, Sagir begged for mercy.

'No! Please! Maqsood bhai! Maqsood bhai! Mercy, Maqsood bhai!'

'Shut up!' Alam roared, and suddenly there was silence. 'Now listen to me, you bastard,' he said. 'Maybe your father will get us for what we did today, maybe the police will catch us, maybe you will come after us. But after today, no innocent girl will ever fall for that pretty face of yours. You know why? Because after today, your face will no longer be pretty.'

Holding Sagar's face firmly under the chin with one hand, Alam proceeded to make several deep cuts on his face before throwing the razor to the ground and breaking Sagir's nose with one forceful blow. His friends then flung the whimpering Sagir to the ground, after which all five of them walked away slowly through the crowd, which parted as they passed by.

Half an hour later, Alam was standing in front of Haji Baba.

'You could have killed him, but instead you meted out a punishment far worse. And you made it symbolic as well. Maqsood beta, well done,' Haji Baba said.

By the time Alam reached home that night, knowledge about his deed had spread throughout the locality. He was no longer the son of municipality-wale Tabrez Alam chacha. He was Maqsood bhai, a name that the unfortunate Sagir had cried out over and over that evening.

By the time he was thirty, the name was almost as big as Haji Baba's. Then his mentor retired, and Maqsood bhai became the king of Dongri. At forty, he was among the most feared gangsters in Mumbai. And at fifty-five, he was running his empire in India while shuttling between Pakistan and the UAE.

Which was why when businessman after businessman started complaining to him about this bloody upstart Shakti Pillai, Maqsood bhai had to sit up and take notice. The same men who were earlier paying up without a single word of protest were now saying things like, 'Bhai, we pay hafta to you but we fear him more.'

Maqsood perceived a threat to his name, one that he could not take lightly. And so he called Sultan Aziz, one of his most loyal and trusted killers.

'Sultan, what is that new craze that the youngsters have these days? The one where they take pictures of themselves?'

'Selfie?' Sultan guessed. He himself was thirty-five years old, although he didn't look older than thirty, and wasn't exactly an authority on these new-fangled crazes.

'Haan, that one,' Maqsood growled. 'I want a selfie of you with Shakti Pillai's dead body. Take another picture of the body we can give to the media.'

Maqsood hung up and speed-dialled Shabbir Khan, his trusted second-in-command. Khan had been one of the friends involved in Maqsood's first murder in Dongri and the disfigurement of Sagir all those years ago. He had stuck by Maqsood since then.

Maqsood told Shabbir to make sure Sultan did not find himself wanting for anything—be it money or any other help—till he had killed Pillai. Shabbir, who had long wanted to see Pillai dead, happily agreed. He also took note of the fact that Maqsood, who usually let Shabbir take care of everything, had personally issued the order to kill Pillai, something that he would make sure he would mention to the media once the bloody mosquito had been crushed.

Sultan, meanwhile, booked himself on the first available flight to Bangkok, which was six hours later. Dipping into his stash of passports, Sultan found one that served his purpose best, one that proclaimed him a Pakistani. He would be posing as a member of a wealthy Pakistani family.

Over the next three hours, Sultan made over fifty telephone calls, patiently piecing together a picture of Pillai's activities in Bangkok. Over the last ten years, Maqsood bhai had developed friendly relations with the underworld in a lot of Asian countries, and Sultan tapped into these contacts, using his boss's name, and watched it work wonders.

The next half hour was spent arranging for weapons to be delivered to him after he landed in Bangkok and a safe house for him to stay. At the end of the fourth hour, he left for the Benazir Bhutto International Airport in Rawalpindi.

4

WHEN SHE FINISHED her study of Pillai's network in Bangkok, Venus had to give a small nod of appreciation. While most Indian gangsters hiding on foreign soil were content with lying low and extorting money from targets in India, Pillai was trying to do something different.

After reaching her hotel in Thonburi, Venus had got in touch with an old friend, a mercenary who now served as a freelance security expert for whoever had the money. As with most mercenaries, he had friends in a lot of places, high and low, and as with a lot of people who had crossed Venus's path and lived to tell the tale, he owed her a favour. Venus liked it when people owed her favours. You never knew when you might need to call one in.

Venus told him what she needed, and within twelve hours, the mercenary—known as Hammer in the shadowy circles she operated in—emailed her a comprehensive report via encrypted email on Pillai's activities in Bangkok ever since he arrived in the city after fleeing India five years ago.

Sitting in a restaurant in Patpong, Venus read the report.

Around a year earlier, Pillai had managed to get an audience with the local crime lord and obtained his blessings to start his own operation in the city in exchange for a hefty cut of his profits. Pillai's men quietly got in touch with hotels and resorts which were run by Indians and roped them in. Some were bought, others bullied, but by the end of three months, Pillai's racket was ready to go operational.

Any tourist in a foreign country naturally feels comfortable and safe when talking to a fellow countryman, and this is what Pillai was exploiting. It remains a fact, to the infuriation of the Thai government, that tourists visit Bangkok less for its Buddhist temples and more for its red light districts. Pillai rented three spaces in Patpong, one of the three red light districts in Bangkok and, with the crime lord's blessing, opened massage parlours in two of them and a night club in the third. His men instructed the managers and senior staff members at the hotels to encourage their Indian patrons to visit Pillai's establishments.

Of course, he was paying through his nose for the local crime lord's continuing patronage, which opened a lot of doors and discouraged the competition. No wonder he needed money, Venus thought, as she finished reading the report. Till business picked up, the money he was making in India was the only major income he had.

Her mercenary friend had sent her addresses of the massage parlours and the nightclub, along with a picture and information about Pillai's frontman for his racket, a Thai national of Indian origin named Raghav Shetty, who was the buffer between Pillai and the law. For all intents and purposes, Shetty owned the three establishments, and would take the fall if something went wrong.

Shutting her laptop and slipping it inside her backpack, Venus looked around the restaurant. It was moderately crowded, as it was lunchtime, and she noted that several of the male customers were obviously pimps.

A waitress came over to ask if she needed anything else, and Venus smiled and shook her head. Five minutes later, she was walking down the bustling street, professional camera in hand, clicking pictures and ignoring catcalls. She was dressed modestly in cargo pants, a loose-fitting shirt and a scarf around her head, but even a casual observer could tell that she was on the voluptuous side, a fact that she had used to her advantage more than once, when the situation demanded it.

She came to a stop near a street sign and leaned against it, pretending to check her camera. The massage parlour directly across the street was Pillai's. She spent a few minutes fiddling with her camera before she once again raised it and started taking pictures while keeping one eye on the massage parlour.

It took her a little while, but she realised that the group of Thai men sitting at a table in an open air café two shops away from the massage parlour were not just lazing around. At any given point in time, one, or two of them, had an eye on the massage parlour. They were security.

Soon, she picked up a pattern. Customers reached the massage parlour in cabs and were accompanied by an Indian man, who would take them inside. The same men would also escort them from the premises after their business was done.

To buy herself more time, Venus pulled out a pack of cigarettes from her pocket and lit one. By the time she finished it, she had confirmed that apart from the Thai men at the café, there was no external security for the parlour. Covertly, she took pictures of the Indian employees at the massage parlour as they entered and exited. She had a hunch that Pillai would trust the Indian members of his gang more than the Thai, and she needed to keep an eye on them.

Venus flicked away her cigarette and followed the street signs to Pillai's nightclub. It was shut, as it was only afternoon, but activity would begin within hours. There was a bored-looking muscular Thai man sitting on a stool by the entrance. But apart from that, Venus could see no other security. Employing the same routine she had outside the massage parlour, Venus took pictures of the nightclub before turning away.

She had nothing much to do for the rest of the day, so she decided to take a walk through the district, taking pictures and thinking about the last time she had been in Bangkok.

In a way, it was funny. It was in Bangkok that she had first taken a human life, a step that had set her on the path from which there was no turning back.

Born into a wealthy, progressive Muslim family in New Delhi, Venus had grown up in luxury, but she had been largely left alone. Her father was a doctor who spent most of the year working at medical relief camps in war-torn regions, while her mother was a professor who could speak six different languages and travelled across the globe for work. Her parents had made sure she received the best education and facilities, but due to their constant absence, she turned into a loner and found solace in literature.

By the time she was ten, she had discovered that she was in love with the Urdu language and spent hours reading the works of Urdu poets and writers. Her parents, particularly her father, wanted her to be physically fit as well, and agreed to hire an Urdu teacher for her, provided she agreed to learn martial arts as well.

For the next eight years, Venus spent her mornings undergoing gruelling workouts and practising hand-to-hand combat techniques with a personal trainer, a well-built man with a stony face and a ponytail. In the evenings, she fell deeper in love with Urdu, with her teacher, the most beautiful woman she had ever seen, gently guiding her.

That changed a little after she turned eighteen. One night, she woke up to see a man standing over her bed. Before she could scream, the man clamped a hand over her face. He was holding a piece of cloth dipped in chloroform, and the smell was the last thing she remembered before she passed out.

When she woke up, she was lying on a bed in a decrepit place, her hands and feet tied to the bedposts and a gag in her mouth. It took her half an hour to stop panicking and calm herself down, after which she did what her father had always told her to do in a tight situation: focus on the solution. It presented itself to her around fifteen minutes later in the form of a nail jutting out of the wall just next to her right hand.

Using all her strength, she stretched her arm enough so that she could rub the rope binding her hand against the nail. Slowly, doggedly, she kept going till, fibre by fibre, the rope began to fray. After two hours, she could free her right hand, and ten minutes later, she had untied her left hand and both legs, and was already on her feet, doing light exercises to bring the circulation back.

The next step was to get out of the shack where she was being held. She tried the door, which was locked from outside. She had no idea where she was or how many people were outside the room she was being held in. She settled down on the floor, just behind the door, and waited. Around an hour later, she heard the door being unlocked. By the time it was swinging open, she was already up on her feet. The man who stepped inside, a parcel of food in his hand, had no idea what hit him when she kicked him, hard, in the back of his neck. He collapsed on the floor, and she used his cell phone to call the police.

The nightmare, however, had only just begun for her. The police officer in charge, despite her demands to see her family, first took her to a hospital for a medical check-up and then to the police station, where he took her to his cabin and asked if he could get her anything.

'My family!' she almost screamed. 'My parents!'

A loud honk brought Venus back to the present. Quickly gathering herself, she hailed a passing cab and went back to the hotel where she was staying.

'Ma'am,' the manager said as she passed by his desk. She stopped.

'This came in for you,' he told her, handing her an envelope. She smiled and thanked him, and waited till she reached her suite to open it. It contained a single key and a piece of paper bearing an address. She pocketed the key, committed the address to memory and flushed the piece of paper down the toilet.

5

As he entered the Royal Thai Police headquarters on Rama I Road in Pathum Wan district in Bangkok, Police Inspector Dayanand Agarkar felt a familiar thrill of anticipation. The same way he had felt years ago when he had been on his way to conduct his first encounter in Mumbai.

A few years after he had joined the Maharashtra Police as a police sub-inspector, Agarkar had learned that, as with any other profession, he would have to be smart in order to survive. With the underworld at its peak in the '80s, Mumbai was a dream posting for any ambitious cop, and Agarkar did what anyone with his resources would have done.

Agarkar's father was a social worker from Amravati and would frequently visit the Mantralaya in Mumbai to seek funding and requisite approvals for his various projects for the upliftment of farmers. Agarkar, whose first posting was also in Amravati, started accompanying his father whenever he could so that he could strike up acquaintances in the corridors of power. After two years of subtle and not-so-subtle lobbying, Agarkar managed to land a posting in the Naxal area in Gadchiroli, a sure-shot booster for a young policeman's curriculum vitae.

Agarkar threw himself into the rigorous training regime that all policemen have to undergo in Naxal-affected areas, and made sure he stayed in the top five in all competitive exercises. As his popularity grew, his superiors started sending him with teams patrolling the riskier areas of the region.

'Be careful,' they warned him. 'A firefight can break out any time.' They had no idea that was exactly what Agarkar wanted.

Six months after his posting in Gadchiroli, Agarkar killed for the first time. It was a routine patrol through a village at night, and there had been no intelligence about any movement in the area. One minute the ten-member patrol was going about its business, and the next they were face-to-face with the enemy.

It was not a planned assault. A group of six Naxals were passing through the area after collecting a consignment of weapons from a gunrunner in a nearby village, and their paths just happened to cross with the patrolling squad. Panicking, the Naxals whipped out the weapons they had just bought and hastily loaded them, while the cops, too, cocked their weapons.

Agarkar was the first to react. Raising his assault rifle, he shot a Naxal right in the face, swung his weapon to the left and shot two more by the time the rest of his squad raised their weapons. The remaining three Naxals were cut down in a matter of seconds, and Agarkar marched into the police station an hour later, his weapon resting on his shoulder, a bag containing the Naxals' weapons in his other hand, to applause from his colleagues.

That day, Agarkar realised two things. First, he loved the taste of victory. And second, taking a human life did not bother him.

After four years in Gadchiroli, Agarkar was ready to move on. Once again, his father's contacts came in handy, and he was transferred to Mumbai, then known as Bombay. He served for two years in the Azad Maidan Police Station before being promoted as assistant police inspector and transferred to the Crime Branch.

There, he found a mentor in his reporting head, Police Inspector Pradeep Shelar, who coached him in the myriad ways of dealing with the underworld. It was also with Shelar that Agarkar conducted his first encounter. It was, ironically, a Shakti Pillai henchman.

Pillai had, at the time, been a recruiter for Maqsood Alam, who had, by then, fled to Dubai. Pillai's job was to find foot soldiers to execute Maqsood's orders, and there was no dearth of poor, young men willing to do anything for a fast buck.

Shelar got a tip-off that one of Pillai's henchmen, Raman Nair, along with some recent recruits responsible for several hit jobs, were going to try and kill an Andheri-based builder at his construction site. Shelar, after getting off the phone with his informant, turned to Agarkar and said, 'Ready for some good work?'

Shelar and Agarkar, dressed in plainclothes, stationed themselves across the street from the construction site. Shelar sat on a plastic stool at a juice and sandwich stall and Agarkar stood next to a cigarette shop a few metres away. Three other constables were waiting in a car around the corner, ready to step on the accelerator.

Just before they left the Crime Intelligence Unit office, Shelar took Agarkar aside and told him, 'Just to be clear, there are going to be no arrests.' Agarkar only looked his mentor in the eye and nodded.

Shelar's tip-off turned out to be right. Roughly half an hour later, a car came to a halt around two feet away from where Agarkar was standing, smoking his third cigarette. Nair stepped out, followed by two others, while the fourth stayed at the wheel, with the engine running.

Shelar was already up and walking towards the car. As the three men started to cross the street, he called out to Nair, who instinctively whipped out a pistol from under his shirt. He was a second too slow. Even as he was raising his pistol at Shelar, Agarkar squeezed off two quick shots from his revolver. Shelar shot down the other two, who also had guns in their hands, while people started screaming and running around them.

Agarkar ran around the car to the driver's side and saw that the man was glued to his seat, both hands on the wheel, trembling with fear. Before he could open his mouth, Agarkar shot him through the half-shut window twice just as the three constables in the car came roaring up to where Shelar and Agarkar were.

Shelar watched in silent approval as Agarkar beckoned the constables over and quickly reached inside the car. Using his gun, he lifted the slumped-over driver's shirt to check for a weapon. On seeing none, he extended his arm and one of the constables slid a country-made gun into his hand. Looking around, Agarkar holstered his own weapon and carefully wrapped the dead man's fingers around the gun before letting it fall. Agarkar had pulled off his first encounter without hesitating for a single second at any point.

Now, as he reached the third floor of the RTP headquarters, Agarkar was thinking of the little tingle that went down his spine when Shelar had told him that there were going to be no arrests. He felt that same tingle right now as he told a uniformed constable that he had an appointment with Narong Anantasu, commissioner of the Metropolitan division.

Agarkar was shown inside within a minute. He entered a tastefully furnished office to see Anantasu, whom he knew from his television interviews, waiting for him with a small smile on his face. Sitting across the table from Anantasu was a man about Agarkar's age and, if Agarkar was reading his face right, of Agarkar's experience and mettle. The man's eyes looked like they had seen death.

'Sit, Mr Agarkar, sit,' Anantasu said genially. 'This is Captain Kaewnan,' he said, gesturing to the other man, who was dressed in a grey suit and white shirt.

Kaewnan turned to Agarkar and nodded. Agakar did the same before turning back to Anantasu.

'I have briefed Kaewnan on the ... purpose behind your visit to our city, and the two of you will be working together.'

'It will be my pleasure, sir,' Agarkar said. Mathur had told him to treat Anantasu with the utmost respect and courtesy.

'Anything you need, you talk to Kaewnan. I have given him authorisation to help you in every way possible, and have provided resources like funding and manpower for a smooth operation,' Anantasu continued, smiling.

Agarkar understood. Anantasu was distancing himself from the operation till it had actually been pulled off. He imagined that Anantasu and Kaewnan had had the same conversation he and Mathur had back in India.

'Understood, sir,' was all he said.

Anantasu nodded to Kaewnan, who stood up.

'Shall we?' he said to Agarkar.

Agarkar stood up and so did Anantasu. Leaning forward, he offered his hand. Agarkar took it.

'Let us do something good together,' Anantasu said, looking into Agarkar's eyes and holding his hand firmly for a second before letting go.

Agarkar nodded. Kaewnan clicked his heels and saluted smartly before turning around. Agarkar followed him to the door. Silently, they exited the building and Kaewnan led Agarkar to the parking lot. Kaewnan unlocked his car remotely and when they reached it, he slid into the driver's seat, while Agarkar went around the hood and got into the passenger seat.

'So,' he said, making an attempt at conversation. 'Where are we going?'

'Suan Luang,' Kaewnan said.

Agarkar had no idea what that was, but asked, 'Why there?'

Kaewnan only smirked and started the car. Agarkar decided not to give him any more opportunities to be smug, and occupied himself by looking out of the window for the rest of the ride.

Less than an hour later, Kaewnan pulled up outside a medium-sized, single-storey warehouse. He pressed a button on his remote-controlled key mechanism, and the single door to the warehouse slid upwards. He drove inside and the door slid shut behind them.

Both men got out and Kaewnan walked over to a corner where he flipped a switch. The lights came on and Agarkar looked around. The warehouse had three tables and several chairs in a corner, along with a large board. Two laptops and a printer were placed on one of the tables, along with stationery.

Another corner of the warehouse had cots with mattresses and pillows, while the third corner had been converted into a makeshift kitchen. Agarkar walked around and saw a large bathroom between the workspace and the kitchen.

He turned around to see Kaewnan smirking at him. 'You did not think we would be running an operation to kill an Indian national on Thai soil from the RTP building, did you, Mr Agarkar?' he said.

Agarkar felt a tinge of affection for the smirking cop.

'So I should check out of my hotel room?' he asked, grinning.

'No, no. We must keep up appearances, no? But feel free to sleep here any time you want to.'

Walking over to the workspace, Kaewnan pulled back a chair.

'I need to make one thing clear, Mr Agarkar,' Kaewnan said.

'Let me save you the effort,' Agarkar said, walking over to where he was sitting. 'Your city, your rules. Close enough?'

Kaewnan smirked again as Agarkar lowered himself into a chair.

'I do not need you to know it. I need you to follow it. If you do not, working together might not be a very pleasant experience.'

'I'd expect nothing else, Mr Kaewnan. I know how this works,' Agarkar said, looking evenly at Kaewnan.

'Good,' the Thai cop said. 'Where do we start?'

Agarkar pulled out his cell phone. Opening his photo gallery, he tapped an image file and handed his phone to Kaewnan.

'I need to know everything possible about this man,' Agarkar said.

6

WORKING FOR MAQSOOD ALAM had its perks, Sultan Aziz thought as he looked at the sunset in the distance.

Sultan had reached Bangkok earlier in the morning and had found one of Maqsood's top men in Bangkok, Zafar Shah, waiting for him at the airport. Sultan followed him out of the airport to a waiting car, which drove him smoothly to an upscale neighbourhood in Sukhumvit. Overnight, Zafar had rented a fully furnished penthouse apartment under the same name that was in Sultan's passport, to fit his cover story of being a wealthy Pakistani on holiday in Bangkok.

By the time Sultan reached the apartment in Sukhumvit, it had been stocked with enough supplies for him to live comfortably without having to step out of the house for a month. Sultan, however, had other plans.

After a long shower, he settled down on the comfortable double bed and soon fell asleep. He slept for four hours before waking up and then made himself a filling meal followed by tea, which he sipped by the window of his apartment while watching the sun set over Bangkok.

It was fifteen years ago that Sultan had first come to work for Maqsood as a bitter, vengeful twenty-year-old. Back then, he had been living a contented existence, managing the chain of three ittar stores that his father, Sohail, a loyal member of Maqsood's gang, had set up in Madanpura.

Sohail Aziz was among Maqsood's oldest aides. He had served Haji Baba as a young lieutenant and happily agreed to be Maqsood's advisor after his first boss retired. At fifty-five, Sohail chacha, as he was known, was the oldest member of the gang and, after Maqsood, his word was law.

It was just after evening prayers on a Friday that Maqsood had called Sultan to his house. Sultan was on his way to one of the ittar stores, as it was peak time for business, and he had only come to the mosque as he had missed afternoon prayers that day. However, Maqsood had never sent for Sultan in the past, and it was with a deep sense of curiosity that Sultan rode his Hero Honda motorcycle to Maqsood's house in Dongri.

Maqsood was sitting by the window when Sultan entered his room. As he walked closer, Sultan saw that Maqsood had tears in his eyes.

'Bhai?' Sultan asked, concerned.

Without turning to face him, Maqsood, his voice breaking, managed to say, 'They got Sohail chacha.'

Sohail felt the ground sway beneath his feet. He was aware of a distinct feeling of cold fury swelling inside him, a fury that he did not even know he was capable of.

Shabbir Khan, Maqsood's right-hand man, came forward and put his arm around Sultan's shoulders. Sultan clenched his fists and willed the room to stop whirling around him.

'Who?' he asked.

'Sultan beta, there is time for that,' Shabbir said.

'No,' Sultan said through gritted teeth. 'There isn't.'

Three hours later, Sultan and seven of Maqsood's best men stood waiting by the edge of the Mumbai–Pune highway. They waited patiently for two more hours, Sultan not saying a word, till a motorcyclist approached them and slowed down near them.

'White Ambassador, five minutes away,' was all he said before speeding off.

Sultan turned around and ducked into the Maruti Van behind him, while his fellow gangsters reached under their shirts and pulled out revolvers. Just as the Ambassador came into view, Sultan stepped onto the road, an AK-56 assault rifle in his hands. An hour ago, Shabbir had reluctantly taught him how to use it.

From the backseat of the car, Ashok Rawle, the undisputed don of Byculla, could only lean forward and stare in shock as Sultan quickly and unflinchingly walked towards his oncoming car. Rawle, a bitter rival of Maqsood's, had for long been trying to eliminate him. Rightly guessing that taking out his trusted advisor would deal a massive blow to the gang's morale, Rawle had sanctioned a hit on Sohail chacha. Four of Rawle's men had gunned the old man down while he was on his way to Maqsood's house after offering afternoon namaaz.

'Run the bastard over!' he yelled to his driver, while his bodyguard sitting beside him whipped out his Walther pistol. He was a second too late. Sultan had squeezed the trigger, and assault rifle bullet rounds were already tearing into the car's front wheels.

There was a horrible grinding noise and the car flipped over, coming to rest in the middle of the highway, wheels in the air. Gasping and coughing blood, Rawle managed to crawl out of the rear left window, somehow scrambling over the horribly mangled body of his guard. His driver had been killed before the car even hit the ground.

Halfway out of the car, he turned around and looked up to find Sultan towering over him. Kneeling, Sultan said in a dangerously low voice, 'Do you know who I am?'

Rawle managed to shake his head. Sohail chacha had worked hard to keep his son away from his work.

'Do you know Sohail Aziz?' Sultan asked.

Around him, his men formed a protective cordon, armed with their revolvers to discourage anyone from taking an interest in the scene unfolding in the middle of the highway. Motorists who approached the overturned vehicle took one look at the armed men around it and sped past without stopping.

'Do you know who Sohail Aziz was?' Sultan asked again.

Rawle, who had gone deathly still, managed to croak out a yes.

Sultan leaned closer.

'He was my father, motherfucker,' he said before extending his hand and grasping Rawle's throat. He squeezed and kept squeezing till Rawle stopped moving. Then he stood up and emptied the remaining rounds in his assault rifle into Rawle's face before walking away.

Sultan drove straight to the cemetery where Maqsood, Shabbir and everyone else were waiting with Sohail chacha's body. He completed the last rights and offered the final prayers for his soul wordlessly. He never set foot inside a mosque again.

It didn't take long for word about Rawle's killing, as well as the brutal and daring nature of it, to spread through the city. Maqsood made sure that many witnesses testified to having been with a grieving, broken Sultan at the time that Rawle was killed, and the case remained unsolved.

Several weeks later, Maqsood and Sultan sat down in the former's' house to have a chat.

'I was much younger than you when I first took a life,' Maqsood said. 'It changes something inside you. Something deep inside. You can either stay on this path, or you can walk away now. I have friends in the Middle East who can help you start a legal business of your own,' Maqsood said.

Sultan was already shaking his head.

'This is my home. These are my people. This is where

I lost my father. If staying here means staying on this path, so be it.'

Over the next fifteen years, Sultan grew to be Maqsood's most trusted and ferocious killer. Word in the gang was that if Sultan wanted someone dead, they died.

The ringing of the doorbell brought Sultan back to the present. Looking at his watch, he smiled. Zafar was efficient.

After a brief peek through the peephole, Sultan opened the door to see a young Thai man standing with a duffel bag in his hand. Without saying anything, the man placed the bag at Sultan's feet, nodded once, and walked away.

Sultan took the bag inside, shut the door, and went to the couch before opening it. Inside there was everything that was needed. He smiled, zipped the bag shut and placed it in the bedroom cupboard before returning to the living room and pouring himself another cup of tea.

His cell phone started buzzing just as he drained the cup. He glanced at the caller ID before answering.

'You ready?' Zafar asked.

'Be down in fifteen minutes,' he said.

Going to the bedroom, he dressed simply but tastefully, looking every bit the wealthy young man on vacation. Locking the door behind him, he took the lift to the ground floor and slid in beside Zafar in the backseat of the car waiting for him.

'Let's do this,' he said, and the car started moving. It was a long drive from Sukhumvit to Patpong—over two hours by road—but Sultan had purposely chosen to have his safe house well away from Pillai's area of operations. Besides, if all went as per plan, he didn't expect to be making this journey more than a couple of times.

The Patpong district was bustling with people by the time his car pulled up outside Pillai's nightclub. Nighttime was business hours here, and it was evident everywhere, be it in the massage parlours, nightclubs or brothels.

A prostitute came sidling up to him as he got out of his car, talking glibly in Thai, but Zafar moved between her and Sultan, shooing her away with a dangerous look. Sultan chuckled inwardly.

There were two bouncers at the door, one a Thai and the other an Indian. Sultan and Zafar had no trouble entering the club, unlike some of the natives who were gathered by the door.

They stepped into the flashing lights of the nightclub, Zafar just ahead of Sultan, clearing a way till they reached the bar. Sultan ordered a beer and swung his barstool around, taking in the scene. Apart from the obviously diverse nationalities of the faces in the crowd, there wasn't much difference between this club and the ones he had been to in India. He had only been inside a nightclub twice in his life, and both times it had been to kill someone.

His beer arrived, and he sipped it slowly, while Zafar stood by his side, playing the role of a rich man's bodyguard well. Even his face, which was normally relaxed and affable, was set into a fixed, menacing expression.

Sultan's survey of the club was interrupted by the sound of someone planting themselves hard on the barstool next to his. He turned his head to see an obviously exasperated woman order a cocktail. She caught him looking at her and nodded in greeting.

'Bad night?' he asked.

She shook her head.

'That's the third man I've walked away from in the last four nights. I don't know why I keep trying,' she said in mildly accented English.

'So, bad nights,' Sultan said.

She nodded morosely as her cocktail arrived.

Sultan thought for a moment. A woman on his arm would make him seem less suspicious if he was going to spend the evening scoping out Pillai's nightclub, and he wouldn't know what to do with a Thai woman. He couldn't place her accent though.

Turning his barstool around, he drained his pint and ordered another.

'I'm Ayaaz,' he said, leaning close to her, giving her the name on his passport.

She ran her gaze from his head to his toe and back, making him feel a little self-conscious, before grinning slightly.

'I'm Saba,' she said. 'Saba Mansoor.'

7

GETTING INTO THE nightclub had been a cakewalk.

After returning to her hotel following her recce of Pillai's massage parlours, Venus had taken a nap. It was early evening when she woke up. She changed into a bikini and headed for the pool area. The hotel had a massive pool, complete with a bar and refreshment services.

Venus perched herself on a barstool and, from behind her sunglasses, patiently surveyed the entire area while sipping on a drink. Fifteen minutes later, the perfect candidate came swaggering along.

He was an American in his early forties, wearing nothing but black shorts and a towel around his neck. *Obviously vain*, she thought as she watched him leering at women in the pool while walking to the bar.

A few moments later, he parked himself on the barstool next to her and loudly asked for a martini.

'Shaken, not stirred,' he told the bartender, before turning in her direction. 'Just like James Bond, eh?' he said to her and winked.

Slipping into the character of an Asian woman

fascinated by white men, Venus giggled a little and said, 'I thought James Bond was English.'

'This James Bond is whoever you need him to be, sweetheart,' he said.

Venus giggled again, leaning forward, showing him some cleavage, and James Bond was hooked.

An hour later, they parted ways in the lobby to go up to their respective suites. James Bond, whose real name was Nathan Hartman, promised to meet her in Patpong later that night and take her to the only Indian-owned nightclub.

He tried hard to invite himself up to her suite right then, but she smoothly put him off, telling him she was expecting some friends from India who also knew her husband.

'I can't wait for tonight though,' she whispered in his ear. She walked away, but not before he had managed to feel her behind.

And so it was that Venus sailed through the nightclub's door on Nathan's arm, wearing a tight black dress that came down to just above her knees, her eyes taking in every detail. Nathan's presence was required, because a woman walking in alone would have drawn attention, which she didn't want.

For the next hour, Venus sipped margaritas in a corner booth, pretending to be hooked onto Nathan's every word, while also identifying the six bouncers keeping an eye on everyone and everything. Three of them were Thai and three were Indian. Pillai was running the place well.

As soon as she felt Nathan's hand running further up her thigh than it had already been, she leaned forward and kissed him on the cheek.

'I'll be back in two minutes,' she whispered in his ear, and let him squeeze her buttock as she slid out of the booth.

She walked towards the restroom but changed tracks midway, slipping through the crowd. She had maybe ten minutes before Nathan got restless and came looking for her, so she moved quickly. It took her two minutes of scanning, pushing through the crowd and warding off advances from drunk men before she finally spotted the two sturdy doors in one corner of the club, the tell-tale sign of where the security hub was based. Everything, from the camera monitors to armed guards on standby in case of a situation, would be behind those doors.

She turned around and started looking for her next target. She found him five minutes later; he was busy conferring with one of the bouncers. His air of importance, obvious Indian features and the deference displayed by the bouncer clearly indicated that he was the manager, and the most important man in the club. Quickly, she slipped her cell phone out of her purse, clicked a picture, and slid it back inside, completing the entire task in a matter of seconds.

Then, she put on her practised drunk expression before starting a teetering walk towards the manager. She paused on the way to lean on a man and exchange a flirtatious glance with him, just for effect, before moving on. The manager had finished talking to the bouncer and was preoccupied with his cell phone when she bumped into him.

The bouncer, who was close by, immediately came over and firmly grasped both her shoulders as she held on to the manager, pretending to sway drunkenly. One second before the bouncer pulled her away, she slid the device into the manager's outer coat pocket.

Slurring her apologies, she let the bouncer lead her away to the restroom. Once inside, she locked herself in a stall and quickly dug into her purse for her cell phone. The device she had slipped into the manager's pocket was a location tracker, given to her by Hammer. She had programmed it to transmit data to her cell phone, and now it showed her that the manager had entered the security hub. Having made sure that it was working properly, she shut down the application, exited the restroom and made her way back to her booth. On the way, she ran into an Indian bouncer, and smiled inwardly at the way everything seemed to be falling into place for her.

'Excuse me,' she said to the bouncer. 'You're Indian, right?'

The bouncer nodded, but cautiously. The rules were very clear about fraternising with patrons. Venus picked up on his diffidence.

'No, no. I just ...' she smiled sheepishly. 'This man I'm with ... well, I just discovered he's kind of a pig, and ... well, I'm sort of worried ...'

The bouncer nodded.

'I'll be around,' he said.

She flashed him a grateful smile and went to her booth.

As she had guessed, Nathan, in her absence, had been steadily getting drunk. As she slid in next to him, he made a wild grab for her, knocking over his drink, and roughly pulled her close to him. She put both her hands on his chest, fighting the impulse to simply snap his neck, and turned her face away as he tried to kiss her.

'Stop teasing me, bitch!' he growled, and she pulled away from him, wearing a shocked expression.

'Nathan!' she gasped. 'How can you talk to me like that?!'

'Oh, shut up!' he snapped, lunging for her again. The next instant, he was almost lifted off the ground by the Indian bouncer. Venus made her hand tremble a bit as she reached for the jug of water on the table and then pretended she was too weak to lift it. The bouncer, still holding Nathan by his neck and one shoulder, caught a waitress's eye and signalled her over. Venus sat down as the waitress poured her a glass of water and accepted it, looking grateful.

'You okay?' the bouncer asked her.

Venus nodded.

Wordlessly, he dragged Nathan out of the club. The crowd parted to make way for them, but hardly anyone stopped what they were doing.

Venus pretended to be in shock for another ten minutes, checking her cell phone once during this time and making sure that the tracker in the manager's pocket was working. She was banking on him not checking his outer pocket at least till he got home. She knew that most men who work in crowded places generally leave the outer pockets of their coats empty. The important stuff goes into the inner pockets and the less important things are usually slid into trouser pockets.

Five minutes later, she was talking to a man at the bar.

'You're from India?' she asked Ayaaz Ali.

'What gave me away?' he grinned.

She chuckled.

'I can spot a fellow Indian anywhere.'

'Oh, you're Indian! The accent confused me,' he said.

'I spent some time in the Middle East,' she said, and her mind suddenly flashed back to the five years she had lived there.

Not now, she told herself, as the images came flooding back. *Focus!*

Ayaaz nodded. 'I live in Pakistan now,' he told her. 'Moved to stay with my grandparents after my father passed away. I now speak Hindi with an accent.'

Venus smiled and slid her stool closer to his by an inch.

She had chosen well, she thought. He seemed decent enough, and she had not caught him looking at her cleavage even once since they got talking. Plus, he'd actually blushed a little when she had very obviously checked him out.

She was not particularly interested in starting anything with him. He was part of her exit strategy after she was done with her recce of the club. She had seen him come in and had also noticed his bodyguard, who was now sitting two stools away, sipping a soda. In case Nathan was waiting outside the club for her, Ayaaz and his bodyguard would be the perfect protection.

Not that she couldn't protect herself, but that would mean blowing her cover. Professional photographers don't usually possess the skills to kill a man in ten different ways, in under thirty seconds.

Back at the hotel, she would have a quiet word with the manager to ensure that Nathan didn't try anything. If he still persisted, well, she would find a way. She always did.

She found herself wishing she had picked up a man who was not staying at the same hotel as her, but she hadn't had the time. In any case, if Nathan managed to get into her room, it would be the worst thing he could possibly do.

Half an hour later, Ayaaz said, 'It's getting too noisy in here.'

Venus nodded. 'I should get going too. I have an early start tomorrow—I want to take some pictures of the sunrise at one of the beaches around the city. Maybe I'll go to Hua Hin.'

'I don't know how you do it,' Ayaaz said, sliding off his bar stool. She saw his bodyguard do the same.

'I could never get up in the middle of the night just to click a few pictures.'

She punched him gently on the shoulder.

'Wait till you see the pictures,' she said.

Ayaaz looked at her for a second, then picked up a paper napkin and asked the bartender for a pen. Jotting down a number on it, he gave it to her.

'I look forward to seeing them,' he told her.

They both smiled. Then he stepped aside to let her pass, after which he followed her to the door.

Outside, they both stopped and turned to each other, while his bodyguard hailed a cab. One drew up next to them almost immediately and they walked up to it. She held out her hand.

'See you again?' he asked, taking her hand.

'See you again,' she said, smiling.

An hour later, she was outside a small rental storage space on Rama III Road. She had gone to the hotel first and asked the cab to wait while she quickly took a shower and changed into a t-shirt, black jeans and a long black leather jacket. She then grabbed the set of keys that the manager had given her in the afternoon and hurried back to the cab, telling the driver where to take her.

It was past midnight, but trucks and cars were still out there on the roads. Nobody gave her a second look as she opened the shutter, slipped inside and closed it. Turning on the lights, she saw that it was everything she needed. Her mercenary contact in Bangkok was really being a great help.

One wall of the warehouse had cupboards, and when she opened them, she saw the shelves were lined with weapons of all kinds, from a six-inch knife to a submachine gun, and plenty of ammo for all the guns. The bottom shelf had what she called odds and ends—wigs, false beards, glasses of various frames, duct tape, screwdrivers, nuts and bolts, and other tools.

The rest of the space was occupied by a car and a motorbike. Behind the vehicles were cans of fuel and engine oil and a complete mechanic's kit.

Venus loaded what she needed into a small backpack—one of the many she found in the bottom shelf—and tossed the backpack into the car. Then she got into the driver's seat, slid the seat all the way back and stretched out on it. She still had time and she was going to need the rest.

8

AGARKAR STRETCHED OUT lazily on the large, comfortable couch in the apartment and smiled to himself.

Things are going nicely, he thought to himself.

It had been three days since his arrival in Bangkok, and the operation against Pillai had begun that morning with a meeting in the warehouse that Kaewnan had rented. The Thai cop had brought along two colleagues, lieutenants Sitthichok Soseetha and Arunee Sukchai. Soseetha was a burly man with a genial smile that could make anyone like him immediately, while Sukchai was a tough-looking woman of medium build with smouldering eyes.

After a quick exchange in their native tongue, the three Thai cops had turned to Agarkar.

'For the remainder of the operation, we have decided to speak only English,' Kaewnan said, flashing his trademark smirk.

'Unless it is to swear at you without your knowledge,' Soseetha added, and everyone, even Kaewnan, chuckled.

On the board in front of the four cops was a photograph of Shakti Pillai. It had been taken by an informant for India's Intelligence Bureau, two years ago, at a private resort in the affluent town of Hua Hin, a few hours from Bangkok. The informant had sent the picture along with a report, according to which Pillai was very careful about his movements and changed homes very often.

'That was two years ago,' Agarkar said. 'After that, his activities increased. He started extorting Indians on a large scale, and is also believed to have been behind six murders on Indian soil, although we don't have confirmation on all six. He claimed responsibility for four of them. We picked up chatter that he accepts contracts on high-profile targets if the money is good—and with these targets, the money would have been very good.'

Soseetha half-raised his hand.

'Maybe that was where he got the seed money for his ventures in Patpong,' he said.

'Could be,' Kaewnan said. 'It would have cost a lot. Buying the property, setting it up, equipment, supplies …'

'Not to mention the hefty payment to Sangsorn,' Sukchai completed.

'Sang … Sangsorn?' Agarkar asked.

'The local crime lord. He owns practically the entire underworld in Bangkok. The other crime families, including the foreigners, all of them, have a standing truce with him. They follow the rules he has laid down strictly—breaking a single rule means cruel and painful death for the offender, coupled with a massive amount of money paid to him as an apology,' Kaewnan explained.

'So Pillai is paying this Songsarn for protection?' Agarkar asked.

'Sangsorn,' Soseetha corrected, smiling. 'And yes. That is why the others don't mess with him. Anyone who works under Sangsorn's hand is automatically immune from attack.'

'From the police too?' Agarkar asked.

Kaewnan sighed.

'Unfortunately, yes. Sangsorn has half the force in his pocket, and has even divided up areas in Bangkok among the cops on his payroll,' Kaewnan said, taking out four photographs from his inner coat pocket. 'For example,' he went on, 'we know for a fact that these four bastards are charged with making sure that none of Sangsorn's establishments in Patpong district are ever troubled. And that includes Pillai's massage parlours and nightclub too.'

Agarkar picked up the photographs and looked at each one of them thoughtfully.

'What kind of resources do we have, Mr Kaewnan?' he asked. 'In terms of manpower?'

'Well, the commissioner has picked out ten officers from various divisions and has sent them on paid leave. They are completely available to us for the duration of this operation.'

'You can trust these people, right?' Agarkar asked.

Kaewnan nodded.

The buzz of his cell phone interrupted Agarkar's recollections. He read the text message and slowly sat up on the couch, after which he waited patiently.

A minute later, he heard the key turn in the latch and Sultan Aziz walked in.

For around ten seconds, nobody in the apartment moved. Sultan stayed rooted to his spot, staring in mute shock at Agarkar. The cop continued to sit on the couch, some fifteen feet from Sultan, holding a Beretta 9-mm pistol in his right hand, which was resting casually on the sofa.

Sultan moved first, whirling around to the door, where he found Kaewnan and Soseetha standing, their pistols pointed straight at him. Soseetha circled around to Sultan's left, gun raised, while Kaewnan came forward till his gun was poking Sultan in the chest. He forced Sultan backwards till he reached the couch, and then gave him a little push.

Sultan fell onto the couch, right next to Agarkar, who put his free arm around Sultan.

'Long time, Sultan,' he said with mock geniality.

Sultan batted away Agarkar's arm from his shoulder. Agarkar calmly placed it on his shoulder again.

Agarkar had seen Sultan at Bangkok's Suvarnabhumi Airport while he was waiting for an RTP officer to meet him. The officer had called Agarkar five minutes after his flight landed and, apologising profusely, told him that his son had been ill that morning, which had delayed him. Agarkar had assured him that it was not a problem, and that he would wait. He had completed the immigration formalities and was roaming about the arrival lounge when he saw Sultan by sheer chance.

Sultan was shaking hands with another man when Agarkar saw him. Recognising his face from an interaction some years ago, he quickly ducked behind a pillar till Sultan and his companion passed by, and then fell into step behind them, keeping a safe distance.

The two men exited the terminal and Agarkar followed suit. Once outside, they walked towards a waiting car and Agarkar walked past them, keeping his head down. He found a newspaper stand not more than twenty feet away from the car, and ducking behind it, he clicked a picture of Sultan on his cell phone just as he was getting into the car, along with the car's license plate.

It was this picture that Agarkar had showed to Kaewnan two days earlier, and that morning, during their first briefing, Kaewnan had produced results.

'Pakistani,' Kaewnan said, laying a printout on the table. 'Holidaying in Bangkok. Family owns an apartment in Sukhumvit, and that car's registered in his name as well. Name is Ayaaz Ali.'

Agarkar smiled. 'No,' he said. 'It's not.'

An hour later, Agarkar and the three Thai cops paid a quiet visit to the building where Sultan was staying. It had three security guards; two at the gate and one inside a cabin. Kaewnan flashed his badge and showed them a picture of their suspect. Both of them confirmed that he had been staying in the penthouse apartment for the last two days. They told the cop that he had stepped out in the evening and got into a friend's car, and was yet to return.

The feeble protests of the guards did nothing to deter Agarkar, Kaewnan and Soseetha from going up to the penthouse suite, while Sukchai stayed inside the cabin with the guards to discourage them from doing anything inadvisable.

Once upstairs, Soseetha, with a smile on his face, pulled out a lock-picking kit from his pocket and the three men were inside Sultan's apartment within a minute.

When Sultan, after being dropped off outside his building by Zafar, walked through the gates an hour later, the guards, under Sukchai's watchful eye, smiled brightly at him while she sent Agarkar a text message informing him about Sultan's arrival.

'So,' Agarkar said, 'what errands are you running for your bhai here in Bangkok?'

Sultan said nothing.

Agarkar sighed.

'Look here, my friend,' he told Sultan. 'That man over there is Captain Kaewnan with the Metropolitan Police, and he is not a very nice man if you get on his bad side. As it is, he's pissed off about you coming to his country on a bogus passport under a false identity. You are, aren't you, Mr Kaewnan?'

Kaewnan nodded, staring hard at Sultan.

'Here's what happens if you annoy me, Mr Aziz,' Kaewnan said. 'All the evidence about your true identity, including your fingerprints from the Mumbai Crime Unit records—'

'Crime Branch,' Agarkar said helpfully.

'From the Mumbai Crime Branch records are in my email already, thanks to Mr Agarkar. It will take me less than half a day to prove that you are Sultan Aziz from India and not Ayaaz Ali from Pakistan. When I do so, I will then throw you in jail and we will start extradition proceedings against you.'

Agarkar took it up.

'At our end, we will spare no effort to ensure that the process goes on as slowly as possible, so that you keep rotting in jail here. The sheer number of murder cases registered against you back home will ensure you don't get bail in the meantime. When you finally do get extradited, well, you're fully familiar with what happens after that.'

Agarkar leaned closer to Sultan.

'And the biggest thing. Your Maqsood bhai will become a laughing stock. Pillai will forever rub Maqsood's face in the fact that he sent his top killer after him, and this infamous top killer got arrested on his third day in Bangkok. Think of how much fun the media will have.'

Sultan clenched his fists till his fingernails were digging into his palms.

'What do you want?' he asked.

'Cooperation,' Kaewnan said. 'We are both after the same man. Mr Agarkar is here to help us put an end to his nonsense once and for all, and unless I am mistaken, so are you. We have our resources, and you have yours. Work with us, and we will personally put you on a flight to Pakistan when it is over.'

'Look, yaar,' Agarkar said. 'You know me. I am happy to bend rules as long as it takes me to my objective. Let's work together. Let's finish off the bastard.'

Sultan was silent, but his mind was working furiously.

'No one can know that I worked with the police,' he said finally.

'Of course not,' Agarkar assured. 'You think we want it known that we worked with a wanted man who was here on a false passport?'

'And what am I going to tell Maqsood bhai?'

'We'll need Pillai alive so Mr Agarkar can take him back to India,' Kaewnan said. It was a lie but he wasn't about to tell a gangster something that only five men in Bangkok, including himself, knew at the moment. 'You can do whatever you want with the rest of his gang and we won't touch you. We will even provide you all the information we have on his gang members. Burn his gang to the ground and go back home a hero,' Kaewnan said.

'Look,' Agarkar said, 'when this is over, I'll get one of my superiors to speak to your Maqsood bhai. One has to make some compromises, yaar. You know how it is.'

Sultan knew only too well what Agarkar was talking about. When he was in Mumbai, he had worked with policemen, once even with Agarkar, to help them finish off members of his rival gangs. Maqsood bhai had told him that he, too, had collaborated with the cops a few times in his life.

'It's about survival, Sultan,' Maqsood had said at the time. 'We do whatever we need to do so that we can survive. If we don't, others will, and all that will remain of us is a handful of dust.'

Sultan had no intention of turning into a handful of dust.

9

'My family!' she almost screamed. 'My parents!'

'Sit down, please,' the officer said.

'No!' she said. 'I am not sitting down. Or doing anything till you take me to my parents.'

The officer sighed.

'Beti ...' he began, and she was suddenly hit with a terrible sense of foreboding.

He sighed again and sat in his chair.

'We got the call at seven o'clock this morning, when your maid let herself in with her key. The house had been looted. Everything that was valuable and could be carried away was taken. She couldn't find anybody in the house and was hysterical by the time we got there.'

She waited.

'We searched the entire bungalow and ... they were in the garage ...'

She couldn't breathe.

'And ...?' she managed to say.

The officer just hung his head.

She screamed.

The swinging doors of the cop's office opened and three constables came running in, while others crowded outside. A female constable gently coaxed her out of the office and into a waiting car, after which she was driven home. Her martial arts instructor, Vikram Khanna, was sitting on the couch, looking like he had aged ten years in a single night. Mutely, she went and sat down next to him. The female constable asked if they needed anything. Neither of them spoke, and the policewoman left wordlessly.

For what seemed like an eternity, mentor and student sat next to each other in absolute silence. Then Khanna leaned forward, placed his right elbow on his knee and rested his forehead on his fist.

'How much did they tell you?' he asked.

'Not much,' she said tonelessly.

He stood up.

'Come with me,' he said.

She didn't move at first. He turned around to look at her.

'Up!' he said in the tone he used during their sessions.

She stood up and followed him.

They first went to her parents' bedroom. He stepped aside to let her enter and stood by the door. The bed was a complete mess. The sheets were on the floor. She let her eyes travel around the room till she saw something that made her stop. Kneeling down, she took a closer look at the stains on the floor. They were of dried blood.

'Four men. Security cameras captured them when they entered the compound,' Khanna said.

'The watchman?' she asked.

'Hit on the head from behind while doing his rounds. He was out cold in the morning when the maid came in. One of the men took you while the other three attacked your parents. Dragged them out of bed and made them open the safe. When your father refused, they started hitting your mother with their bare hands till he begged them to stop and complied.'

She felt her blood turn to ice.

'Do you want me to stop?' he asked her.

Somehow, she didn't.

'They took them to the garage, locked them in there, and then cleaned out the rest of the house. The exterior camera caught a tempo outside. Then they went back to the garage for your parents,' he went on.

'How did they die?'

He gestured for her to follow him, and they headed down to the garage. The floor was covered in blood stains.

'Post-mortem report says blunt force trauma to the head and broken bones all over,' he said quietly.

She walked around the garage. When she reached the tool shelf, she saw that the biggest hammer on the shelf was missing.

A muffled groan snapped Venus out of her thoughts. She turned from the window where she had been standing and smoking a cigarette, and smiled.

'You're awake,' she said.

The manager of Pillai's nightclub in Patpong struggled to get off his chair, only to find his legs bound to it, while his wrists were duct-taped to the dining table in front of him. He moaned through his gag again, slowly regaining his senses.

After putting together the equipment she would need in the garage, Venus had slept till her cell phone's alarm woke her up at dawn. She slipped on a wig with dreadlocks, a dense false moustache and covered her eyes with black sunglasses. Her long leather coat would hide her figure and unless she had to speak, the disguise would hold. Fifteen minutes later, she was driving to Patpong, and an hour after that, she was parked across the street and a few feet away from Pillai's nightclub.

She waited patiently for more than an hour, smoking the occasional cigarette as the nightclub emptied out, till the manager finally walked out and got into his car. She smiled. He drove his own car, which meant there were no inconvenient drivers to take care of.

She let him drive past her and then followed him. Twice she lost sight of him, but the tracker that she had slipped into his pocket guided her, and she soon found him again.

After a forty-five-minute drive, she watched as he drove up to a moderately expensive mansion with a small garden and a porch. She smiled again. A privately owned house was always better than an apartment building.

She kept driving till she found a parking space. She looked around to make sure no one could see her before she took off her wig and moustache. She tied her hair into a bun, pulled on a red wig, wore a pair of round glasses and slung a camera around her neck. As she got out of the car, she put the backpack over her shoulders. Her transformation was complete.

She walked back to his house, clicking pictures of the surroundings when she passed by morning walkers, who smiled at her. At his gate, there was a security camera; she was sure there would be others, but those weren't going to be a concern.

She pulled out a handkerchief from her backpack and wiped the buzzer after she had pressed it. A few minutes later, she heard his voice.

'Yes?' he said.

'Hi ...' she began, making sure she sounded as Indian as possible. 'I ... I'm a tourist and my car broke down ... can you help, please?'

After a short pause, the manager said, 'Are you from India? You sound like it.'

She smiled brightly.

'Oh wow, you too?' she asked.

There was a beep and the gate's electronic lock clicked open.

'Suswagatam.'

She gave a short laugh before walking in.

By the time she had walked up the driveway to his door, it was open and he was standing inside, wearing a t-shirt and shorts, looking tired.

'I hope I didn't wake you up or something ...' she began as she reached his door.

He shook his head and opened his mouth to say something. At that exact instant, Venus shot her right hand out, jabbing him in the throat with her fingertips. He stumbled backwards, clutching his throat, and she followed him inside, pushing the door shut behind her.

'Oldest trick in the book and you just fall for it like that,' she said as she found his jugular vein and depressed it. 'Men will be men.'

He took nearly an hour to come to, and during this time, Venus—now wearing gloves—bound and gagged him, made a round of his house to confirm he was alone, and retrieved her tracking device from his coat, which was flung on his bed.

Now, as the manager—whose name, she had learned during her search of the house, was Rajeev Bhandary—came to terms with his situation, Venus pulled up a chair and sat across the dining table from him. She raised her right hand and showed him the meat cleaver she had taken from his kitchen.

'If I take off your gag, you have to promise not to shout. If you do, the gag goes back on and I chop off a finger.'

Bhandary could only nod, his eyes wide with terror. Venus had to chuckle. The man worked for a notorious mobster but was clearly just a manager, not a gangster.

She pulled off the gag and Bhandary took a few deep breaths through his mouth before speaking.

'You ... who are you?' he asked.

Venus made a face.

'I thought I had a memorable face. And you saw me from pretty close last night,' she said.

Bhandary only stared uncomprehendingly.

Venus sighed.

'I'll take care of my bruised ego later. For now, let's talk about Shakti Pillai.'

Bhandary started to sputter. Venus held up a hand.

'If you lie to me, your fingers start coming off. I have no reason to hurt you unless you give me one, and no one has to know you talked to me. I'll leave as quietly as I came, and you won't ever see me again.'

The manager pressed his lips together, sweat running down his forehead in small rivulets. Shaking her head, she leaned forward and pushed the gag back in his mouth, stood up and walked around the table till she was next to him. With deliberate slowness, she gripped his right hand, while the other hand raised the meat cleaver.

Bhandary suddenly started shaking his head very hard, trying to say something. Venus looked at him, meat cleaver still raised, and said, 'Stop moving,' in a deadly whisper that made the man freeze in a second.

'If you're willing to talk, nod once,' she said.

Bhandary nodded once.

Venus smiled.

Going back to her chair, she sat down and then, reaching across, pulled the gag out as Bhandary's breathing came back to normal.

For thirty minutes, Venus listened patiently and attentively, asking several questions, as Bhandary painted a picture of Pillai's activities for her. Most of it she already knew, thanks to Hammer's report, and she made a mental note to tell him he had done an excellent job.

The one point that stood out throughout Bhandary's narration was that the man at the centre of it all was Raghav Shetty, the frontman who, on paper, was the owner of the two massage parlours and the nightclub.

'Also, the businesses are kept separate,' Bhandary said. 'For example, say you want some cocaine to go with your drink. You will be taken out and led to a den two buildings away where you can get your fix and then be brought back by the same Thai staff at the club. Selling inside the club is strictly forbidden. If a customer is caught with drugs inside the club, it's the customer who suffers. But the entire purchase and supply of the drugs is managed entirely by Thai players. No Indians, including me, are connected to it at all.'

'So in case there's a bust in the club ...'

'I can very safely claim innocence, at worst accusing the Thai waiters and bouncers of running the racket on their own, because there will never be any evidence to tie me to it. The Thai get the drugs from their own suppliers, and everyone, from the movers to the dealers, is Thai.'

'So, the Indian players are well protected,' Venus said.

Bhandary nodded.

'And the Thai members are okay with that?'

Bhandary shrugged.

'They're paid well. And with our contacts in the police, the possibility of them being caught is next to nil.'

'How do I get to Pillai?' she asked.

Bhandary stiffened at the mention of Pillai's name.

'I have been working for him for nearly a year now, and I have never even spoken to him on the phone, forget seeing him. I keep hearing about some right-hand man called SP, but again, I have never seen him. Everything is handled by Shetty, and we don't even meet him that often. I met him when he hired me, and then when there was a problem with the club's accounts. Works the same way at the massage parlours. We only meet him if something goes wrong,' he said.

Venus smiled.

'Something like his nightclub manager getting killed?' she asked.

10

FOUR HOURS AFTER the little chat between Agarkar and Sultan in the latter's penthouse in Sukhumvit, the four policemen on Pillai's payroll were quietly put under surveillance.

The ten officers that Anantasu had put on standby were roused out of their beds at four in the morning with orders to get to the warehouse within the hour. Once there, Kaewnan quickly briefed them about their tasks. Apart from Pillai, the board now also bore pictures of the four corrupt cops.

'We need to keep an eye on them at all times, see who they meet in Pillai's gang. As part of their services to the gang, they will visit the massage parlours and the nightclub every once in a while. They will also meet someone in the gang to collect payment. Follow them, get pictures of the people they meet,' Kaewnan instructed.

He then split the officers into five teams of two, and assigned one team to a corrupt cop, with the fifth team on standby.

'Each of you will take turns watching your target while the other rests. You can work out your own systems of division of hours,' he told his men. To the standby team, he said, 'I want you two available at all times, in case you need to replace someone, or something else needs to be done.'

All the officers nodded and murmured their assent.

Kaewnan turned to Agarkar.

'Anything else?' he asked.

'It might be a good idea to dress a bit more casually,' Agarkar said, looking at the men and women in their crisp formalwear. 'And let the beards grow out,' he told the six men on the team.

Kaewnan nodded.

'Good input,' he told Agarkar, who chuckled.

'Like you wouldn't have told them yourself,' he said.

Kaewnan looked at him.

'I know when I'm being tested, Kaewnan,' Agarkar said.

The ten cops dispersed and Kaewnan and Agarkar turned back to the board and the pictures on it.

'You think Aziz will stay in line?' Kaewnan asked.

'He has to,' Agarkar said. 'He's been fiercely loyal to Maqsood. Making him lose face is not something he would want to do, even though it wasn't actually his fault we traced him. Had I not seen him at the airport ...'

Kaewnan nodded.

Before leaving from Sultan's apartment, Agarkar had given him a cell phone.

'Keep this on you at all times,' he told Sultan. 'Use this to call me.'

Sultan nodded. 'What about Zafar?' he asked.

'Tell him nothing. He can be useful as a resource, but I don't trust him not to go blabbering to Maqsood.'

Sultan finally agreed, and as soon as the cops left, Kaewnan told Soseetha, who was also the team's technical expert, to track the location of the cell phone Agarkar had given Sultan at all times.

Soseetha and Sukchai walked into the warehouse then, carrying parcels of food.

'I hope you don't mind burgers,' Soseetha said. 'The least crowded place I could find at this time was a Burger King.'

They all took chairs around one of the tables and passed the burgers, fries and sodas around. Once they were settled in, Kaewnan turned to Agarkar, who nodded and placed a laptop on the table, its screen facing the other three.

'Just got this from my colleagues back in Mumbai,' he said. 'This man,' he said, pointing to a picture on the screen, 'is Pillai's right-hand man and bodyguard rolled into one.'

Everyone leaned forward to take a better look.

'His name is Sharad Pillai, but he's better known as SP.'

'Are they brothers or something?' Sukchai asked.

'No, no. It's a common surname. The name Pillai represents a community.'

The Thai cops nodded, and Agarkar went on. 'SP was one of Pillai's very early recruits. They grew up together, and when Maqsood Alam recruited Pillai, he took SP with him. Their job was to recruit fresh blood for the gang's myriad jobs.'

'Pillai worked for Maqsood?' Kaewnan asked.

'Oh yes. Long back, when Maqsood was still in Mumbai. Maqsood fled to Dubai in the late '90s, taking only his trusted few with him, like Shabbir Khan and Sultan Aziz. Pillai gathered whatever men he could and tried to run his own gang in Mumbai.'

'But?' Sukchai asked. Agarkar flashed her an impressed look. She was good, he thought.

'But the Mumbai Police had finally had enough by then. Gang members were being shot down on sight and Pillai realized he wasn't as big as he thought, and that he could easily be found dead in some lane one morning. So he fled to Thailand on a false passport, and ultimately ended up here.'

'And this guy came with him?' Soseetha asked.

'He was the only one who did. He has two enforcers in Mumbai who take care of the groundwork over there, but Pillai and SP pretty much run the show from here. Over the last couple of years, they've reached out to small-time Indian criminals here and managed to form a network that runs the massage parlours and nightclub, I'm told.'

Kaewnan nodded.

'Checks out with what I'm hearing. But my sources say this is just the beginning, that Pillai is planning to expand his activities,' he said.

'If that is true, he will need more seed money,' Sukchai said.

Agarkar nodded thoughtfully.

'And that means more people in India might suffer soon. Or get killed, if Pillai takes a contract.'

All the four cops pondered this for a minute.

'Right,' Kaewnan said. 'The priority is to get to either SP or their frontman, Raghav Shetty, as soon as possible.'

'Yeah, tell me about this Shetty character,' Agarkar said, picking up his burger.

'He's a local businessman,' Kaewnan said. 'Came to Bangkok around two decades ago, got a Thai citizenship, and settled here. He had some family money, which he invested in a couple of businesses. Grocery store, restaurant, then a garments store. Then, a year ago, he started those massage parlours and the nightclub in Patpong. In fact, till he did that, no one had even heard of him,' Kaewnan said.

'Yeah,' Soseetha agreed, his mouth half full. 'Before that, he was just another rich man getting richer while the poor got poorer. It was only after he opened those three places that we took note of him, as we do with everyone else who has establishments in the red light districts.'

'Let's get back to SP,' Sukchai said, picking up her Pepsi. 'Any current information on him?'

'Scant,' Agarkar said. 'Indian intelligence reports place him with Pillai. He never leaves his boss's side, which is natural since he is a bodyguard, and Pillai is said to trust his judgement. SP is also the one who gets things done for Pillai, be it getting someone's phone or email account hacked, or hiring private investigators to shadow targets. Pillai and SP are supposed to have thought up this whole new-age crime between themselves.'

'Well,' Soseetha said. 'What do we do?'

'You said something about hiring private detectives?' Sukchai asked.

Agarkar nodded.

'There has to be a phone trial, right? I mean, someone has to have called up the private detectives to hire them? Could we get call records?'

'We could. But it might not lead anywhere. My guess is that the detectives are hired by someone working on Pillai or SP's instructions, either here or in Mumbai. The SIM cards used are most probably destroyed as soon as the job's done. Pillai himself would probably contact the guy using internet calls, which can't be traced anyway.'

'Can you still get the phone records of the detectives hired by Pillai's gang? I have an idea,' Sukchai said, picking up a French fry.

'Sure,' Agarkar replied. 'I'll get it done.'

Sukchai smiled at him and bit into her fry.

After they were done eating, Sukchai went over to the laptop. Tapping a few keys, she printed out a copy of SP's picture and three copies of the dossier on him. By the time Soseetha and Agarkar came back to the table, Sukchai had pinned SP's picture on the board right next to Pillai's, while Kaewnan had placed the copies around the table, one each for himself, Soseetha and Sukchai to take home that night and study.

'What specifics do we have on this Shetty?' Agarkar asked as they settled down around the table again.

'Basics,' said Kaewnan, lighting a cigarette. He slid the pack and his lighter across the table towards Agarkar before continuing. 'Registered address, vehicle records, tax returns. No criminal record. Travels a lot and is not seen often. Has a wife and kid who stay here. She spends his money by the truckload, while the kid is a typical over-pampered, overweight brat.'

'Not bad,' Agarkar said, before he realised what he was saying. 'Oh, I meant these cigarettes!' he clarified, looking at the name of the brand on the pack. 'So,' he went on, 'is Shetty in the country now?'

Kaewnan shook his head.

'He's in Australia for a business meeting.'

'Can we quietly put out an alert so we know when he comes back? Without setting off any alarms?'

'I know a person who works with airport security,' Sukchai said, getting up and pulling her cell phone out of her pocket.

'What else can we do?' Agarkar asked Kaewnan.

The Thai cop thought for a minute.

'For Shetty, I guess we need to wait for him to come back. I'll get his phone records in the meantime. For Pillai and SP, I think our surveillance is our best bet.

Let's see who my four esteemed colleagues meet for their bribes, and maybe we can start tracking them as well. Someone, somewhere, has to be meeting Pillai and SP.'

Agarkar grinned.

'It all comes down to patient, dogged hunting, doesn't it?'

Kaewnan nodded.

'Detective work is detective work, regardless of where it happens.'

'We should also be ready to move in at a moment's notice as soon as we get word on either SP or Pillai, boss. Who are we going to involve at that point?' Soseetha asked.

'No one,' Kaewnan said. 'We do this ourselves. The commissioner will take care of jurisdiction and other headaches after it's done.'

Agarkar's cell phone rang. He checked the caller ID and instinctively stood up while answering it.

'Sir?' he said.

'How is it coming along?' Mathur asked, his voice sounding strange.

'It's coming along, sir. We're working on it aggressively.'

'Well, be more bloody aggressive, will you?' Mathur said, and Agarkar suddenly realised that his boss was sounding strange because he was furious.

'Sir, kya hua?' he asked.

'Check the bloody news,' Mathur said and hung up.

The three Thai cops had seen Agarkar's face change and looked at him enquiringly. Agarkar sat down on a chair and pulled a laptop towards him. Typing quickly, he ran a news search on Google for Shakti Pillai. Everyone came around to his side and leaned forward as they went through the search results together.

Sukchai was the first one to respond.

'Seed money,' was all she said.

11

VENUS TOOK A sip of her iced tea as she listened intently to the video playing on her laptop.

She had returned to her hotel late in the evening after her visit to Bhandary's house. She had taken a hot shower, letting the heat soak in through her pores, after which she had slipped on a loose t-shirt and shorts, crawled into bed and gone straight to sleep.

When she woke up, it was late night. She called room service for a smoked chicken sandwich and a jug of iced tea. It was while she was finishing her sandwich that she got the alert on her cell phone.

After she took on the hit on Pillai, the first thing she did was to read up all available material on his activities, including the latest news reports about him. She then set up an email alert for any news item regarding him, so that she would get a notification in her email as soon as an article was put up on any news portal. It was this notification in her email that interrupted her dinner and she put her plate aside, powered on her laptop and opened her mailbox, by which time she had several more links in her email.

She went through the short takes on newspaper websites one by one, and all of them had pretty much the same thing to say: IAS officer Aslam Soorti shot dead by gangster Shakti Pillai's men.

She went back to her sandwich. The first one hour was going to be a barrage of information, much of it speculative and unverified, and she knew that she would have to wait for a while till in-depth, substantiated reports started coming in. She finished her meal and drank a glass of the mint-flavoured iced tea before she turned back to her laptop.

She then looked up television news websites till she found a live broadcast video of the report. Pillai had called up a senior reporter with the channel and confirmed that he was responsible for the murder. The reporter, with full consent from a willing Pillai, had recorded the entire conversation, which was now playing on the broadcast.

'Yes, yes. My men only killed Soorti,' Pillai was saying.

'But why?' the reporter asked.

'What do you mean "why"? There was a hit on him. He had made many enemies. It was an open hit. So I took it. Never mind that I'm not in the country. I still have my ways.'

'So, you're saying you did this only for money, not out of personal enmity?'

'Look, boss. Don't give me that principles wala funda. That went out of fashion long ago. If I have the means to kill someone in India while sitting here, and if the money is good, I will do it, okay? And this is nothing. Now just wait and watch.'

'Are we to assume that there will be more such contract killings in the days to come?'

'You assume anything you want. Okay, I'm hanging up now.'

The conversation was replayed thrice, with the anchor yelling himself hoarse about how spineless and incompetent India's law enforcement agencies were, before signing off by promising a full panel debate on the issue in an hour.

Venus closed the link. She had heard enough. Refilling her glass with iced tea, she sat back in her chair to think. Pillai had made a career out of extorting businessmen and killing some of them for money. But this was the first time he had killed a government servant, and a senior one at that.

Gangsters, including Maqsood Alam, who were still extorting businessmen in India, worked in accordance with an unspoken brokered agreement with the law enforcement machinery. There were certain things that the police allowed them to do, and others that the gangsters were absolutely not supposed to do. Like touching someone in the government.

Pillai breaking that rule either meant that he had never had any such arrangement with the establishment in the first place, or that he had become daring enough—or desperate enough—to break it.

In either case, it increased the need for him to be put down as soon as possible. Fortunately, Venus thought, she had already set the wheels in motion.

✦

Sultan and Zafar were in the living room of the penthouse in Sukhumvit, a cell phone on the glass table in front of them. Sultan was sitting calmly, one leg crossed over another, while Zafar was pacing up and down behind him, wiping the occasional drop of sweat from his forehead.

An hour ago, Zafar had reached Sultan's apartment and leaned on the doorbell till Sultan, who was in the shower at the time, had come to answer the door, dripping wet, with a towel wrapped around his waist. Zafar followed him to the bedroom and waited while Sultan went back to the bathroom to dry off and put some clothes on. As soon as he emerged, Zafar told Sultan about the call he had received from Shabbir Khan, Maqsood's right-hand man.

'That fucker killed an IAS officer. You've heard of Aslam Soorti? Maharashtra cadre. He was pretty senior in the PWD and impossibly honest. Shot down a lot of applications for government tenders because the applicants weren't honest enough. Everyone tried to drum some sense into him, but it was no use,' Zafar said.

'What happened?' Sultan asked.

'He was out with his wife and son in Bandra. In some fancy restaurant. Pillai's men simply walked in, shot him point blank and ran away. His kid got blood all over his face.'

Sultan shook his head.

'Poor kid,' he said.

Zafar scowled.

'Fuck the kid!'

Sultan eyed him dangerously. Zafar cowered.

'I'm sorry, yaar. I ... I just ... I'm sorry. It's just that, you know, we have bigger worries right now.'

Sultan turned around and walked to the living room. Zafar followed him.

'Shabbir bhai sounded really angry. This goes against all the rules, yaar! Soon the bastard's going to be giving more interviews to news channels. It's going to be bad for business too.'

'What else did Shabbir bhai say?'

'That I should come to you with a new phone and stay here till Maqsood bhai calls.'

'Then I guess we should just wait, shouldn't we?' Sultan said, settling down on the couch.

The call came half an hour later. The cell phone on the table buzzed. Zafar made a dash for the table, but Sultan scooped it up and answered it.

'Hello?' he said.

'As-salaam-o-alaikum,' came Shabbir's distinct growl from the other end.

'Walekum assalaam, Shabbir bhai.'

'How are you, Sultan beta?'

'I'm good, bhai.'

'Wait. Maqsood bhai would like to talk to you,' Shabbir said.

Five seconds later, Maqsood was on the line.

'Sultan,' was all he said.

'Salaam, bhai.'

'Salaam. Beta, what are you doing?'

'Bhai, I understand your anger. But acting in haste will only lead to losses. It's only been four days since I got here. Please trust me. I am working on this.'

There was silence. Then Maqsood spoke.

'Beta, you wouldn't be there if I didn't trust you. But this changes things. He is getting out of hand.'

'Or maybe he is digging his own grave, bhai.'

Another short silence.

'Explain,' Maqsood said.

'Bhai, he might think he is being brave. But what if he is just becoming more and more cocky? Arrogance always leads to downfall. If he can be stupid enough to kill a government servant, with a little pressure, he might be arrogant enough to show himself. That is exactly what I was working on anyway, on smoking him out.'

'You think you can do that?'

'I am already working on it, bhai. I was just getting the lay of the land before making my move. Zafar is with me. He will make sure I have everything I need. Believe me, bhai, very soon you will see results.'

Sultan waited with bated breath.

'Okay, Sultan. But soon,' Maqsood said.

'Inshallah, bhai. Very soon.'

'Destroy this phone and SIM card.'

'Of course, bhai.'

Zafar heaved a huge sigh of relief as Sultan ended the call and handed him the phone. Although he didn't show it, Sultan was immensely relieved himself.

Zafar kept blabbering as he dismantled the cell phone and removed the SIM card. Sultan waited till he had flushed the SIM card down the toilet and thrown the pieces of the phone in the trash.

'It's getting late,' Sultan said. 'Get some sleep. We have work to do tomorrow.'

Zafar looked at him curiously.

'You have a plan?' he asked.

Sultan winked and smiled. 'Trust me,' he said.

Zafar nodded and left. Sultan waited for ten minutes, then walked swiftly to the bedroom. Raising the mattress on the bed, he picked up the cell phone that Agarkar had given him.

✦

Sitting in the warehouse in the industrial district of Bangkok, Agarkar, Kaewnan, Soseetha and Sukchai read copies of the report that Mathur had emailed Agarkar fifteen minutes ago. It was a report that Mathur had personally written, and it included alerts on the wireless radio from the time the shooting was reported to the control room as well as updates from the concerned police station and the Crime Branch chief.

They all finished reading the report around the same time, after which they sat in silence for half a minute.

Soseetha was the first to speak.

'Damn,' he said. 'In front of his wife and thirteen-year-old son!'

'You knew the man?' Kaewnan asked Agarkar.

'Knew of him,' Agarkar replied. 'Maniacally honest. With a man like that, any number of people could have put out the hit.'

There was silence for another minute.

'Seed money,' Agarkar said finally, looking at Sukchai.

They all nodded.

'He's starting something here. Something new. Maybe another nightclub or casino or something completely illegal and secret. And we need to find out what that is. I'll speak to the commissioner,' Kaewnan said.

'What are the chances we'll actually get to know what he's planning before he does it? Realistically?' Agarkar asked.

There was a moment's silence. Agarkar knew that this was an important question. Kaewnan could either choose to defend the image of his police force by displaying misplaced trust in its capabilities, or he could look at the larger picture.

Every other cop in the room realised the same thing, and all eyes were on Kaewnan.

'Realistically? Slim,' he said.

Agarkar looked at Kaewnan with respect. *It must have taken a great deal to be able to admit that in front of a police officer from a foreign country*, he thought, and wondered if Kaewnan was just following Anantasu's orders or if he really wanted to do some good.

'If I'm right,' Kaewnan went on, 'he's already paid off more cops, and with Sangsorn behind him, I really can't be sure of anything.'

There was a pause.

'But?' Agarkar and Sukchai said at the same time, and took a moment to smile at each other.

'But we're tailing those four cops we know are on his payroll. And if we play this right, we might be able to get enough leverage on one of them to squeeze them into giving us information. It might cause a stink if it gets out that the cop is on the payroll of the underworld don, but if we are to cause some serious damage to Pillai, this is the best way.'

'Say we do get to know what he's planning,' Agarkar said, 'what do you suggest we do?'

Kaewnan turned to Soseetha.

'Are you still as good with explosives as you used to be back when we worked together?' he asked.

Soseetha smiled. 'What do you need, boss?'

'Just start getting the material from your contacts,' he said.

Soseetha stood up, pulling his cell phone out of his pocket, and walked to a corner.

'Want to tell me what you're planning?' Agarkar asked.

Kaewnan just smiled.

'I know that smile,' Sukchai said. She was smiling too.

12

SHAKTI PILLAI TOOK another long gulp of his beer and sat back in the easy chair, a contented smile on his face.

Raising his legs, he crossed one over the other on the table in front of him. His wife used to scold him for this habit back in India, telling him he would ruin the table. He would try telling her that he could buy her ten more, but she would never listen.

'There is no need to throw away your money,' she would say, and he would just smile.

For a moment, a shadow fell over his mood. It had been five long years since he had seen her. The last time they met, SP, his trusted lieutenant, had sneaked her into Phuket using a false passport. They had spent three blissful days together before he had to return to Bangkok to take care of business.

Soon, he thought, he would get her and his son to Bangkok for good. He just had to establish himself a bit more.

The key was to convince Sangsorn that he was here to stay. The crime lord had been sceptical, almost dismissive, when Pillai had first approached him. Pillai had to practically beg him for a chance, and that was something he had not done since he had approached Maqsood for a job, back when he was a young tough on the streets of Andheri. He hadn't disappointed Maqsood then, and he assured Sangsorn that he wouldn't disappoint him.

The thought of Maqsood further dented Pillai's upbeat mood. He had served Maqsood loyally, and while he always knew that Maqsood would sooner or later have to shift base out of India, he had expected to accompany his boss when he moved. Instead, he was fed a crock of shit about what a big responsibility Maqsood was giving him by leaving things in his hands. Even a child knew that anybody who got left behind was simply expendable.

Well, he thought, *Maqsood made his choice, and I made mine.*

Thanks to SP, Pillai had realised what an important role the media could play in his life. He had observed carefully as the media chronicled tales of Maqsood's exploits, and knew that no news was bad news for reporters. The police struggled in vain to keep the media from glorifying criminals, but very few journalists could resist the opportunity to put out an eyeball-grabbing headline or TV news flash, no matter what the cost.

Over the last five years, he had successfully ensured that every threat call he made, every life he took and every target he otherwise hurt, was credited to him.

'Sooner or later, the police are going to slap a case against you. Claim credit before that. Let the people know it's you. Keep them scared,' SP had told him, coming up with the brazen idea of calling up news channels to claim credit for a job after it was done. There were times when the police had registered cases against him after watching news programmes featuring his telephonic interviews.

The police kept saying that every call he made to journalists to claim credit was an admission of guilt and would go against him when he was finally nabbed. When he heard this, Pillai laughed. He had greased enough palms in Bangkok to be able to receive a heads-up the minute the Indian government tried to get him extradited. The ever-trusty SP had an emergency exit plan ready, just waiting to be executed. Now, with Sangsorn's protection, he had become even more untouchable.

It was also SP who had given him the idea of having a frontman for his illegal activities in Bangkok, so that he was not a criminal on Thai soil. His arrangement with Raghav Shetty was simple: Shetty would be swimming in money as long as he took care of Pillai's illegal activities, and if he ever got arrested, Pillai would bear all his legal expenses and spend whatever amount of money was needed as bribes to get him off, while also taking care of his family. An added incentive was the threat that Pillai had coldly issued on the day that he and Shetty had made their agreement.

'You breathe a single word about me to the police, and I'll kill your wife and son before I leave Thailand. I'll also capture it on camera and send a copy to news channels,' Pillai had told a sweating Shetty.

His cell phone rang and he absently reached for it while taking another gulp from his mug. It was an unknown number, but the prefix on the caller ID told him that the call was from Australia.

'Hello?' he said.

'It's me.' Shetty was on the other end, his voice sounding strained.

'Bol.'

'Bhandary's been killed.'

'Who the fuck is Bhandary?'

'Our nightclub manager,' Shetty replied, his voice shaking a bit.

Pillai felt the buzz from the beer dissipating.

✦

'A robbery, apparently,' Soseetha was telling Agarkar and his two colleagues at the warehouse.

'What was taken?' Kaewnan asked.

'A lot of stuff, according to the report. The safe in his bedroom was broken open. The local police did not find any cash at all in his house. It seems to have been cleaned out. The tan line on Bhandary's wrist indicates he wore a wristwatch, but that wasn't found anywhere in the house. The house itself was in a mess, but they can't say what was taken because Bhandary lived alone and there's no one else who can give a proper inventory.'

'Did the house have any security cameras?'

'One. Over the gate. But whoever did it took the recorder with them, so it's useless.'

'Any other cameras in the area?' Sukchai asked.

'Some,' Soseetha replied. 'They're looking at the footage.'

'Cause of death?' Agarkar asked.

'Asphyxia. But he was roughed up a bit before he was strangled. He was found tied to a chair and his hands were duct-taped to the dining table. He had also been hit several times in the face and one of his ribs was cracked. He seems to have been hit with something hard and blunt.'

'Not punched with bare hands?' Agarkar asked.

'Autopsy report says no,' Soseetha replied.

'You'll keep getting updates?' Agarkar asked Kaewnan, who nodded.

'The commissioner will pass on everything to me the minute it comes to him. We're good on that front.'

Sukchai's cell phone rang. She stepped aside to talk.

'What are the chances it's not actually a robbery?' Agarkar asked Kaewnan and Soseetha.

'I don't know,' Kaewnan admitted. 'If it's someone who is going after Pillai, it would have to be that Sultan of yours. And we've been tracking his cell phone's location. We also put his man's cell phone under surveillance … I forgot his name.'

'Zafar. And you're right. They haven't been anywhere near Bhandary's residence. If the two of them didn't do it, there's either some new player we don't know about, or it was genuinely a robbery.'

'It's not all that improbable, boss,' Soseetha said. 'The organised gangs would be aware of Sangsorn's protection, but some of the others might not. Pillai is still a relatively new player, and it takes time for word to spread. It could be some local gang looking for a fast buck.'

'Also, if this were a gang killing, they would want it to look like one, not like a robbery,' Kaewnan reasoned.

At that moment, Sukchai came back to them, sliding her cell phone in her pocket as she approached.

'Raghav Shetty just booked a flight to Bangkok from Australia. He lands in twelve hours,' she said, smiling.

Kaewnan punched his thigh softly.

'At least some good is coming out of this,' he said. 'Who can we get to follow him as soon as he lands?'

'How about I do it?' Agarkar suggested. 'I've done it before and I'm less likely to arouse suspicion, posing as a tourist, than any of you guys. This man is a priority target and we can't lose him.'

'Perfect,' Kaewnan said.

'I'll send you his flight details,' Sukchai said.

Agarkar nodded his thanks and turned back to Kaewnan.

'Did you ever watch that movie *Sholay*?' he asked. 'Any of you? It was huge in India when it released in the early '70s, and is still a classic.'

The three Thai cops nodded. Indian movies were a rage in other Asian countries as well.

'Jai and Veeru,' Soseetha said, smiling broadly.

'What about it?' Kaewnan said.

'There's a line that Thakur says. *Loha garam hai, hathoda maar do*. Basically, a good blacksmith strikes while the iron is hot.'

'Okay ...' Sukchai said.

'How about we add to Pillai's problems?'

'How?' Kaewnan asked.

Agarkar pulled out his cell phone.

'It's time Sultan made himself useful,' he said.

✦

The young Thai man stepped out of the restaurant, humming to himself. He was on schedule, and if he finished in time, he would be able to see his girlfriend tonight. Her parents were out of town and were returning late at night. If things went smoothly, he could drop off the consignment, collect his payment from the nightclub, and be at her place in an hour.

Still humming, he walked to the parking lot and waited by his car for two minutes, pretending to be checking his phone. Then, glancing around to make sure no one was watching, he walked around to the trunk and opened it. He had left it unlocked before going into the restaurant to use the restroom and, as promised, someone had opened the trunk in his absence, placed two duffel bags inside and pressed the trunk shut.

For a moment, he marvelled at the system Pillai had set up. Every week, he would drive to a restaurant well away from Patpong, making sure he got there in the lull between lunch and dinner time. He would park his car in a secluded corner of the parking lot, which would usually be behind the restaurant, and leave the trunk unlocked. Next, he would enter the restaurant and ask to use the loo while his supplier's men placed the drugs in his trunk. Then he would drive back to Patpong and deliver the drugs to the den near the nightclub, collect his pay, and leave.

The man was so engrossed in marvelling at the efficiency of the racket that he did not notice a moderately built man with dreadlocks and a moustache walk up to him.

Without breaking stride, Venus, sweating a little under the fake dreadlocks, pulled out a silenced Beretta 9-mm pistol from under her long coat, raised it and fired thrice. She was beside the delivery boy by the time he started slumping forward.

Holding the lid of the trunk with one hand, Venus shoved the boy inside the boot, bringing him to rest in an awkward foetal position around the two bags. She went through the boy's pockets, found the car keys and slipped them into her bag. She then closed the trunk, got into the driver's seat and started the car.

13

Ranjit Bakshi could not suppress a smile as the cab made its way through the traffic in New Delhi, hardly a kilometre away from his destination.

The Maharashtra cadre IPS officer had retired as director general of the Maharashtra State Security Corporation, regarded by everyone, including him, as an extremely unworthy end to a career full of achievements and accolades.

If there was one word that anyone could associate with Bakshi as a policeman, it was 'legend'. His entire career was dotted with operations that were any cop's envy. After the mandatory postings in rural areas as sub-divisional police officer and assistant superintendent, Bakshi had got his first brush with fame as superintendent of police with the Nashik Rural Police. Unlike in city commissionerates, where an SP-level officer is a mere DCP in the pecking order, in rural commissionerates, an SP is the overall head. Along with power, the position brings with it the responsibility of an entire district, and only the wise can handle it well.

Bakshi was nothing if not wise. Two months into his posting, a ten-year-old girl was found raped and murdered in a farm under his jurisdiction. While the doctors at the local government hospital conducted a post-mortem examination, a huge crowd of villagers gathered outside. Two hours later, her parents marched to the SP's office, her father holding the little girl's heavily wrapped body in his arms, followed by hundreds of villagers. They refused to move. Before any of his subordinates could do anything, Bakshi stepped out of his office, wearing a simple white shirt and grey trousers, and walked straight to the parents.

'I have a daughter,' he told the broken man softly. 'She is four years old. If something happened to her, I would probably set the city on fire. That you have come to the system for justice makes you a better man than me.'

Bakshi watched the father intently as he spoke.

'I promise you I will do everything in my power for the sake of little Pooja,' he said, and her father's face started crumpling.

A few minutes earlier, Bakshi had called up the inspector in charge of the concerned police station and got the dead girl's name from him.

'But for her sake, I must ask you for one thing: take her to the cremation ground. Let her have the last rites she deserves. Mourn her while I go after those who did this to her.'

Pooja's father crashed to his knees, her body still in his arms, and started weeping bitterly. Bakshi gently took the body from his arms and stood up. The father wiped the tears from his face and stood up as well. Bakshi started walking, followed by the girl's father and everyone else behind him, including scores of policemen.

Bakshi walked straight to the cremation ground where he stopped and turned to Pooja's father. Respectfully, gently, he placed the girl's body back in his arms.

'The next time I see you,' Bakshi said, 'I will have either caught those who did this to her or I will have resigned.'

Stepping back, he turned around and walked away, followed by his men.

Of course, Bakshi had no intention of resigning. He had already asked the inspector to start watching all the young men, right from early teens to those in their late twenties, that the girl had come in regular contact with. Constables in plainclothes had kept an eye on all the girl's neighbours even at her cremation. Go for the obvious suspects first, was a rule drilled into them at the training institute.

Meanwhile, another team of policemen visited the girl's house and fanned out from there. Bakshi himself rounded up some of Pooja's friends even as her body was placed on the funeral pyre, and gently coaxed details of her daily routine from them. After an hour of patient questioning, with the help of two female constables, one of the kids finally remembered that Pooja was seen going into a neighbour's farm the previous day. Five more minutes of questioning revealed that the neighbour had two sons, both in their late teens.

Bakshi, along with ten of his men, scoured the entire farm till they found a girl's brass anklet in a small hut meant for storing farming supplies. He called up one of his cops at the funeral and gave him precise instructions, after which he left for his office.

After the funeral, five of Bakshi's burliest cops stationed themselves at the gate of the crematorium and waited till the two teenage boys came up to Pooja's father to pay their respects. As they turned and walked out of the cremation ground, the five cops—who were in plainclothes—started following them, making no attempt to hide their presence.

The two teens cast several looks over their shoulders, and then exchanged glances with each other, their pace quickening with each step. It didn't take long for the other villagers to notice the spectacle and they started drifting over to them, curious, which only scared the boys more.

They cracked in less than two minutes. Suddenly, without warning, they turned around and threw themselves at the feet of the cops following them.

Yes, they screamed, almost crying, they did it. Yes, they would confess, they said, and begged the cops to take them away before the villagers tore them to shreds with their bare hands.

As if on cue, a sixth policemen came roaring up to the spot in a police van. The boys were bundled into the vehicle, which sped to the nearest police station.

The villagers ran behind the van and the police were able to push the boys inside the police station just before it was surrounded by furious villagers, thirsty for the boys' blood. Just when it seemed that they would tear the building down, Bakshi's cavalcade arrived, sirens blaring. The sight of Bakshi walking to the cremation ground with Pooja's body in his arms was still fresh in the people's minds, and they parted to make way for his vehicle.

Bakshi stepped out in full uniform, looking furious, baton in hand, and stormed into the police station before anyone could say anything to him. Within a minute, the sound of blows, along with both the boys crying out in pain, started ringing out of the open windows. The villagers' angry protests died down quickly, and for several minutes, all anyone could hear was the boys begging for mercy.

Five minutes later, Bakshi came out, missing his cap and baton, face glistening with sweat. The people could only watch him, their thirst for blood quenched by the screams of the boys. He stepped right into the crowd and started walking to his vehicle without saying a word. Pooja's father was standing near it, hands joined, tears streaming from his eyes.

The next day's issue of several local newspapers had two photographs—one of Bakshi walking to the crematorium with Pooja's body in his arms and the other of her father standing in front of him, hands joined.

From then on, there was no looking back, as Bakshi solved case after case wherever he went, successfully playing on the emotions of people to ensure that he was hailed as a hero. His smart detection methods and clever manipulation of people and media alike soon brought him to Mumbai as a DCP, and he never served anywhere else after that. From DCP, he rose through the ranks to additional director general, doing a ten-year deputation with the IB during this time, and ultimately achieved his dream of becoming Mumbai police commissioner.

Then the government changed. And so did priorities. While the earlier government was perfectly happy to let Bakshi play to the gallery as long as he solved crimes and got things done, the new government wanted its own men in key spots. Within months of the new government being formed, rumours of Bakshi being replaced started doing the rounds. Bakshi wasn't worried.

'I achieved everything that I had to the day I sat on this chair,' he would tell his journalist friends. It wasn't arrogance. Bakshi felt secure in the knowledge that no ADG-level officer had the merit to replace him. And he was right. Among his peers, he truly was the first among equals.

What he didn't count on was how far the government was prepared to go in order to weed out the obstacles in its path. One fine evening, while on his way home, Bakshi received a text message from the chief minister.

'Congratulation on your promotion to DG. You will head the Maharashtra State Security Corporation from tomorrow.'

And that was it. He had been shunted to a side posting via a text message, while the government placed an officer from a minority community in the Mumbai police commissioner's post, thus ensuring minority votes for the next election. What these stupid voters did not realise, Bakshi thought furiously, was that their beloved hero of the community was due to retire in two months. And two months later, Mathur, who had been the government's choice for the post since it came to power, was appointed without any debate.

Bakshi spent the next one year heading the MSSC, which provided paid security to various institutions, before he retired. After which he found himself slipping steadily into depression. He was drinking more than he used to, he hardly went out and he didn't speak much with his wife and children either.

And then, a week ago, he saw it. His chance to get back. Back in the limelight and back at all those who had laughed at his misfortune, not always behind his back.

'What do you mean "why"? There was a hit on him. He had made many enemies. It was an open hit. So I took it. Never mind that I'm not in the country. I still have my ways.'

'So, you're saying you did this only for money, not out of personal enmity?'

'Dekh, boss. Don't give me that principles wala funda. That went out of fashion long ago. If I have the means to kill someone in India while sitting here, and if the money is good, I will do it, okay? And this is nothing. Now just wait and watch.'

Bakshi was making himself his first scotch and soda of the evening when he saw the interview on the news. His wife and children had headed out for the weekend to Matheran, and he, as he had been doing a lot lately, asked them to go without him. This time they hadn't even argued.

As the interview came to an end, Bakshi put down his glass; he hadn't taken a single sip. He had had countless brushes with Shakti Pillai and his men in the course of his career and had not taken him seriously. He thought of Pillai as one of the many wannabes who were trying to make a name for themselves. Now he wondered if he had made a mistake.

Picking up his glass, he took it to the kitchen and threw its contents into the sink. Then he went to his bedroom and dug around in his cupboard till he found what he was looking for. When his family returned late at night, they found him sitting on his bed, surrounded by his famed diaries. Bakshi was known to have written detailed accounts of his work on a daily basis in leather-bound diaries; he had a diary for each year. By the time his family returned from their trip, it was close to dawn and Bakshi had gone through half of them.

'Did you sleep at all?' his wife asked him.

'Who's got the time to sleep, woman?' Bakshi asked with all of his old joviality. 'There's work to be done.'

As the cab drew to a halt, Bakshi chuckled, remembering the look on his wife's face. He picked up the briefcase he had brought with him. Thanking his driver, he got out and paused to look at the grand Central Secretariat building before walking through the entrance. He patiently went through the security check and then walked to the Ministry of Home Affairs department.

'Ranjit Bakshi, retired IPS,' he said, smiling. 'I have an appointment.'

14

As he left his hotel in Thonburi in a cab, Nakul Gupta could not help feeling excited. The twenty-year-old was on his first solo vacation abroad and, so far, it had been nothing but wonderful. He had spent his first two days in Bangkok visiting the floating markets and the Buddhist temples before finally working up the courage to ask the manager about the 'nightlife' scene.

The manager, after watching Gupta shuffle and stutter, finally got the idea and smiled. Taking Gupta aside, the manager said, 'I know a man who can help you out with that sort of thing.'

'He's … it's safe, right?' Gupta asked.

'Do not worry, sir,' the manager replied. 'He's Indian.'

That reassured Gupta somewhat and he waited eagerly to hear from this Indian.

The next morning, there was a discreet knock on his door and Gupta opened it to see the manager standing outside with another man, who was clean-shaven and obviously well off. He was dressed simply, in an open neck shirt, trousers and leather shoes, and exuded confidence.

'I heard you're looking for a tour guide,' he said, grinning. 'I'm Rocky.'

That afternoon, after a delicious lunch of local sea food, Rocky and Gupta got into a comfortable car waiting for them and started towards Patpong.

'Excited?' Rocky asked.

Gupta, who had been taking in the sights through the car's window, turned to Rocky and nodded, smiling.

'I … I've never done this before. I'm not sure …'

'Don't worry,' Rocky said. 'Whatever you need, you get, as long as you pay. Just meet your masseuse and take it forward from there.'

Gupta nodded, and five minutes later, they were outside one of the only two massage parlours that, according to Rocky, were owned by an Indian in Bangkok.

Rocky and Gupta had stepped onto the pavement and were about to enter the massage parlour when a car came to a screeching halt right next to them. Gupta saw Rocky's hand fly behind him, while at the same time a masked man leaned out of the front window, a submachine gun of some kind in his hand, and fired a single burst in Rocky's face.

Gupta stood rooted to the spot as Sultan Aziz coolly stepped out of the car.

'Run away,' was all he said.

Gupta was more than happy to comply and started running without looking back.

Two stores down, a group of seven Thai men sitting at the open air café sprang into action, whipping out pistols from under their loose-fitting shirts. They never had a chance. Zafar Shah had parked his car across the street from them ten minutes earlier, and now he stepped out, gun in hand, wearing a mask of his own. Between him and Sultan, they cut down all seven men in less than a minute.

Sultan ejected the clip from his Mac-10 and rammed home a fresh one just as two armed men came running out of the parlour. Without hesitating, he shot them both down. Looking at the panic spreading around him, he reached into the car and came out with three canister-shaped hand grenades. Quickly pulling the pins, he tossed one through the door, then shot out the glass panes of the window and lobbed the other two inside, counting the seconds in his head.

Then he turned and ran towards Zafar, who was already back in his car, pulling out into the street. Sultan slid into the front passenger seat and Zafar turned the car around with a screech of burning rubber. He stepped on the accelerator just as the street shook; there was a series of explosions.

Ten minutes later, Zafar and Sultan discarded the car, which was stolen, parking it at a busy intersection near Patpong, and switched to another one. An hour later, Zafar was dropping Sultan at his apartment building. Sultan made his way up to his apartment with a smile on his face. As soon as he entered, he went to the bedroom, pulled out the phone Agarkar had given him, and made a call.

'Bol,' Agarkar said, picking up on the third ring.

'It's done,' Sultan told him.

'Good. Call your bhai,' Agarkar said before hanging up and tossing the phone on the seat beside him. Easing his foot on the accelerator, Agarkar let another car come between him and the one with Raghav Shetty in it, who had landed at Suvarnabhumi Airport an hour ago.

✦

'Arrey chhodo,' Shabbir Khan said, 'are we not capable of killing people there while sitting here? Why do people respect us? Any problems they have, they come to us and not the police.'

'Are you saying that the settlement of disputes with the underworld's help, which used to happen earlier, is still happening?' the reporter asked.

'Look, young man. It has always been happening. As long as we are settling business disputes peacefully and without any bloodshed, even the police don't have a problem. People respect us. That is why they listen to us when we settle their disputes. It's when dishonourable people like this Shakti Pillai start shedding blood simply for personal gain that there are problems.'

Khan was talking to the same journalist that Pillai had spoken to after he'd had Aslam Soorti killed in Bandra.

'But Pillai has a different opinion on these matters,' the journalist said.

'I couldn't care less about his opinions. All I can say is—and he will understand this if he is half as smart as he claims to be—a candle always burns the brightest before it goes out,' said Khan.

In his Bangkok villa, Shakti Pillai threw the remote control at the TV set, missing it by inches.

Half an hour ago, he had learned about the attack on his massage parlour. Then the Thai man who ran the drug racket at his nightclub had called, telling him that a delivery of twenty kilograms of cocaine had never made it to the drug den, and neither had the delivery man. Just as he got off the phone, he saw the interview on the news.

As he struggled to bring his breathing back to normal, he heard SP enter the room. Without saying anything, SP picked up the remote and sat down on a couch.

'What the hell is happening, SP?' Pillai asked.

'We're under attack,' SP said calmly. 'It's not something we didn't think would happen.'

'It wasn't supposed to happen!' Pillai snapped. 'This is exactly what I'm paying Sangsorn for.'

SP nodded. 'And that's protecting you from the local competition. You think someone like Maqsood cares about pissing off a local crime lord in Bangkok? Sangsorn won't be able to get anywhere close to Maqsood without being butchered.'

Pillai took a deep breath as he got up and started pacing. There couldn't have been a worse time for things to start going wrong, he thought. He was funnelling all his money into a new venture in Bangkok in partnership with Sangsorn. A partnership with the crime lord himself would put him in the big league in the Bangkok underworld, and he would never have to worry about anything after that.

Shetty, who was going to own the new venture on paper, was running around to make sure everything was above board and legal. Pillai was pouring every dime from the massage parlours, the nightclub and his extortion racket into the venture, and a loss in revenue was the last thing he needed right now.

Which was exactly what was happening, he thought angrily. First the attack on the massage parlour and then the drug consignment disappearing. On top of which he was going to have to look for another manager for his nightclub who was as trustworthy as the last one.

'So what do we do?' he asked.

'We get ready. If they've attacked once, they will attack again. But this time, we'll be ready.'

'I can't afford to take this sitting down, SP,' Pillai said. 'I can't appear weak.'

'I know that, bhai. I know that,' SP assured him.

'Hit them back. And hit them where it hurts,' Pillai said.

'I have a plan,' SP replied.

Pillai nodded and turned away. SP stood up and walked out of the room, slightly irritated. He hated it when his boss stated the obvious to him. SP was practically managing the whole show, and was well aware of what Pillai could or could not afford.

✦

Venus was impressed as she went through the false trail that the hacker had created. Although she had a fair idea of how hacking worked, she marvelled at the way hackers could create entire identities on the internet in a matter of hours. The hacker she had hired had concocted a very legitimate-seeming identity for her and set up a company in her name, emailing her everything in three hours.

Venus transferred the amount they had agreed upon to the account specified by the hacker and wrote him a short email of appreciation. Then she turned her attention to the task at hand. In quick transactions of different amounts, she deposited fifty million US dollars to the account that the hacker had set up in the name of her new identity. Then she logged into her newly created email account and started typing.

✦

Raghav Shetty had just reached his house in Rangsit when his cell phone beeped. He allowed himself a hot shower and wrapped himself in a robe before checking it.

He read the email twice and sat down on a chair in his bedroom, thinking for a long time. Then he went to his study and, opening the bottom drawer in his desk, removed a stack of SIM cards. Inserting one in one of the three cell phones in the same drawer, he called Pillai.

'How desperate are we for money?' he asked the gangster.

'What the fuck does that mean?'

'An Indian woman named Maya Sahani has contacted me. She's looking to invest her money and apparently trusts Indians over the natives,' Shetty said.

There was silence.

'What do you think?' Pillai asked.

'At the very least I think I should meet her and see how much money she's talking about. If we play this right, I might be able to get enough out of her to cover our recent losses and not let them affect our latest venture.'

'Speaking of the latest venture ...'

'Everything is falling into place,' Shetty said. 'We just need to ensure the money doesn't stop coming. Apart from expenses, there are also a large number of palms to be greased.'

'I know that!' Pillai snapped.

'So, what do we do about the woman?' Shetty asked.

'I'll think about it and let you know,' Pillai said before hanging up.

15

SHE WALKED AROUND the garage. When she reached the tool shelf, she saw that the biggest hammer on the shelf was missing.

She turned around to face Khanna, her eyes blazing.

'How did they get in?' she demanded. 'How did they disable the alarms? They must have had the codes for that. How? HOW?'

Her martial arts instructor sighed, running a hand through his long salt and pepper hair.

Her father, in keeping with his cautious nature, had installed intruder alarms in the house, and the sirens would have woken up the entire neighbourhood. They could have only been disabled by someone who knew the codes. Apart from her parents and the watchman, only Khanna and her Urdu teacher, Shabnam Mukhtar, knew the codes.

She walked up to Khanna till her face was inches away from his.

'Who was it?' she asked simply.

'Shabnam's fled the country. Cops found out an hour ago that she took a flight to Thailand last night,' he said.

She took a step back and, for an instant, her beloved teacher's gentle face with its benevolent smile flashed in front of her eyes.

'Shabnam didi?' she said, shocked. Stumbling, she made her way to a bench in the garage and sat down, shaking.

Khanna went over and sat next to her.

'Why?' she finally managed to ask.

'I don't know.'

After another moment's silence, she asked, 'Did they catch the men?'

'Only the one you attacked. The other three are missing.'

'Is he saying anything?'

Khanna looked at her.

'They didn't tell you?'

'They haven't told me anything,' she snapped.

'He's in a coma. Looks like you kicked him pretty hard.'

'I meant to.'

She stood up and started pacing. Khanna watched her for a minute and then said, 'Come with me.'

He led her to the terrace of her bungalow where her father had set up a gym and training area for her. Khanna tied his long hair into a ponytail and took off his shoes. She did the same.

For the next forty-five minutes, mentor and protégé duelled hard. She used all the martial arts techniques he had taught her since she was ten years old, till she began to tire out. Finally, she was bending over, hands on her knees, breathing hard. In spite of everything, she was feeling fine.

Without saying anything, she turned around and went to her room. Stripping, she stepped into the shower and let the hot water wash over her for a long time. Then she dried off, slipped on the first t-shirt and shorts she could find, and collapsed into her bed.

When she woke up, the next day was dawning. She had slept for over twelve hours. She wandered through the empty house, half hoping that Khanna had stayed back so that she would have someone to talk to. But he was nowhere to be seen. She went back to her room to get her cell phone to call him.

She saw that she had missed several calls from friends and acquaintances. Apart from her parents, she didn't really have any family to speak of, save a couple of distant relatives who lived abroad. She scrolled through the alerts till she saw an unread text message from Khanna. He had sent it late the previous night. It only said, 'There's food in the fridge. I'll be in touch.'

A knock on her door interrupted Venus's recollections and she went to open it. It was nearly noon and she was still in her hotel room because she did not have much to do at the moment. It was room service, and she let the boy set the food on the table in the living room and tipped him generously before shutting the door.

Walking back to the table, she picked up the remote and switched on the television. She was flipping through the channels, looking for something interesting to watch, when she saw a familiar sight and paused. It was a local news channel running a story about an attack on a massage parlour in Patpong. She caught a glimpse of the name above the massage parlour, which confirmed her suspicion. She didn't understand what the anchor was saying, but she didn't need to. The visuals on the screen showed several dead bodies with obvious bullet wounds, and the shattered remains of the massage parlour. Venus had thrown too many grenades in her career not to recognise the damage caused by one.

She watched intently as the camera panned over the scene, showing another group of bodies outside a café two shops away.

She picked up her phone and called Hammer.

'Took you long enough,' he said, answering the call on the fourth ring. 'Saw the news?'

'Yeah,' she said. 'You picking up any buzz about it?'

'Naah. I first thought you were behind it, but you usually work alone, so ...'

'So no idea who it might have been?' she said.

'No. See, that's what's interesting. If it had been a local player, there'd have been some chatter about it by now. There isn't. Plus, none of the locals are crazy enough to go after someone under Sangsorn's protection.'

'You'll let me know if you hear anything?'

'Sure.'

'Thanks, Hamm,' she said before ringing off.

Picking up her plate, she started eating, her mind sifting through possibilities. If, as Hammer said, the local gangs hadn't done it, that meant there was a new player in the game. Which meant she had competition. It also meant that, with someone else attacking Pillai, he would get desperate sooner than she was expecting and was likely to take the bait she had dangled before him in the form of an investment opportunity.

Unfortunately, she did not have the luxury of sitting and waiting. It was time for the next step of her plan.

16

MOHSIN SAYYED WAS a happy man.

For the world in general he was a middle-aged accountant, crunching numbers by day and going back to his family at night. Only a select few knew what he actually did cooped up in his office in Mumbai Central all day long.

He was thirty years old when he was first introduced to Maqsood Alam. At the time, he had been just another chartered accountant struggling to survive in a saturated industry. Sure, he was great with numbers, but so were many others.

A Mumbai-based businessman who was one of Alam's financiers had approached him to get some tax work done. Sayyed quickly realised that large sums of money were unaccounted for, and it did not take him long to figure out where they were going.

However, Sayyed had been hired for a job, and he knew that if he did it right, it might be his entry into a world full of money and opportunities. The law was not something that Sayyed held in high regard, and in any case, he was only laundering money, not taking a life, he reasoned.

The businessman was so impressed by Sayyed's whitewashing of his finances that he kept Sayyed on a retainer. Soon, other businessmen who were associated with Alam started hiring him, and Sayyed was in business.

The turning point came when, at a New Year's party, one of his patrons took him aside and handed him a phone. At the other end was Maqsood.

'I hear you're doing good work,' Maqsood said.

'Shukirya, bhai ...' Sayyed managed to say.

'Keep it up. I am sending you a small gift.'

'Ji ... ji, bhai ...'

The call ended before Sayyed could say anything else.

The 'small gift' was a place on the board of directors of a real estate firm that was a front for Maqsood's activities in Mumbai. All the extortion money from builders and film stars was funnelled through this firm's accounts before being dispersed to other firms run by Maqsood in Dubai.

As a director, Sayyed was given access to the company's bank accounts and the responsibility of improving the laundering process. No one understood exactly what it was that Sayyed did, but by the end of the year, the process was much smoother and faster. Sayyed even found a way to invest some of the money in a few lucrative places and turned a profit on them.

He now lived in a plush house in Bandra and travelled by car every day.

That evening, he had dispersed another large amount that the firm had earned in profit to three Dubai-based firms. On his way home, he received an email. It was from a chartered accountants' body that he was a part of, and the subject line read 'Invitation for Annual Function'. Sayyed chuckled. Five years ago, no one had cared to invite him anywhere. He opened the email and saw there was a formal invitation attached. He downloaded and opened it, taking note of the time and venue. He would reply in the morning. There was no need to seem eager by replying immediately.

He reached home, had dinner with his wife and daughters, spent an hour going over his daughters' homework and then retired for the day, happy and content.

He woke up the next morning to a call from one of his employees. It was a routine matter. A payment had to be made earlier than usual. Sayyed said he'd do it himself. Quickly, he accessed the banking app on his cell phone, logged into the company's account and transferred the amount. Then he shut the application and went to have a bath.

By the time he got ready and checked his phone, he had several notifications, including two unread text messages. His attention automatically went to the text messages because they were from his bank. He opened them and felt his blood run cold.

The first one informed him that his net banking password had been changed as per his request. The second one announced that his registered mobile number had been changed, also as per his request.

With trembling fingers, he called his bank and spoke to his relationship manager. By the time he finished the conversation, he was sweating profusely.

✦

'Tell me exactly what happened,' Shabbir Khan said on the phone.

Sayyed took a deep breath.

'After I saw the messages, I called the bank and they told me that someone had logged into the company bank account using the right login and password, after which they first changed the password and then the phone number in the bank's records. After that … after that, in some thirty transactions, a total of seventy-five crores was transferred to various accounts.'

There was silence.

'Where did the money go?' Shabbir asked.

'To accounts all over the country. I don't know what happened to it after that. But the banker told me that if I did not make those transactions, chances are that someone hacked into my account. I asked him how it was possible, and he put me in touch with an expert in these matters. I … I didn't want to involve the police.'

'Good thinking. What did this expert tell you?'

Sayyed gulped.

'Apparently an email I received last night, from what I thought was an accountants' association, carried a virus. It was programmed ... as in, it was made in such a way that it would only capture the keys I pressed on my phone when I opened my net banking app and send that information to the hacker.'

Pillai, Shabbir thought immediately. If it was a hacker, it had to be Pillai's doing.

'What happened next?' he asked.

Sayyed gulped again.

'Apparently someone tipped off the cops. A couple of them landed up at the office while others went to the bank. The fellows at the bank were bound to cooperate, so they got enough to start a primary inquiry. And whoever tipped them off specifically mentioned Maqsood's name, so they're taking it seriously. The ... the company's transactions have been stopped and accounts have been frozen till the inquiry is complete.

'I'll be in touch,' Shabbir said before ringing off.

✦

Three hours later, Shabbir was speaking with an officer in the Cyber Crime Investigation Cell, who was on the gang's payroll. He confirmed what the expert had said about the virus.

'It's called a trojan,' the officer said. 'You think it is one thing, but it is actually something else. In this case, the hacker set up a fake email account in the name of the accountants' association, and sent the virus disguised as an invitation. The minute Sayyed operated the company's bank account from his phone, it captured the login ID and password. The rest was easy.'

'What about the money?'

'Transferred in various small amounts to accounts in Noida. The money was further transferred in smaller amounts to other accounts. My guess is that it will be withdrawn from multiple ATMs within the next couple of days.'

'And you can't stop it?'

'We'll be lucky if we can identify the accounts before the money is withdrawn and disappears.'

Khan ended the call abruptly, grinding his teeth. He hoped Sultan was hurrying up with whatever he was working on. Maqsood bhai was not going to be happy.

17

As is mostly the case with good old-fashioned police work, results took some time to come, but they did come.

It had been fifteen days since Agarkar and Kaewnan had begun their joint operation, and twelve days since Kaewnan had put the four Thai policemen on Sangsorn's payroll under surveillance. Every night, Kaewnan's team would email pictures of the four cops, from the time they left their houses to the time they returned.

'Use your judgement,' Kaewnan had told them. 'I want pictures of whoever they are meeting. Send them to me and we'll see who we can identify.'

After Sultan and Zafar attacked Pillai's massage parlour in Patpong, Kaewnan asked the officers tailing the corrupt cops to inform him the minute any of them went to the location.

True to his hunch, one of them, Somchai Meesang, reached the scene within half an hour. Kaewnan's surveillance team called it in and Kaewnan told them to take pictures of whoever he met after leaving. Two hours later, Kaewnan had several pictures in his inbox.

After leaving the massage parlour, Meesang had got into his car, driven a short distance, and met a Thai man at a restaurant. Kaewnan smiled. He recognised the man from his time in the Crime Suppression division. He was one of the top drug runners for Sangsorn and had a lengthy record to his name.

And so, that evening, Metropolitan Police Commissioner Narong Anantasu called Meesang to his office for a quiet chat.

'This picture,' Anantasu said coldly, showing him the photograph of him meeting Sangsorn's drug runner, 'can destroy you. You are five years away from retirement. Your disgusting corruption apart, you have some good work to your name. Everything will be shattered if this picture makes it to a single newspaper in Bangkok. And if you don't think I will do it, watch me.'

Meesang was sweating.

'Unless you do exactly as I say,' Anantasu went on, 'you are finished.'

Wiping the sweat from his bald head, Meesang started talking, unaware that Kaewnan was listening to every word from inside Anantasu's antechamber.

After nearly an hour of grilling, Anantasu was done with Meesang.

'Get out,' he told his subordinate. 'And do not breathe a word of this to anyone, least of all your criminal friends.'

It was late evening when Kaewnan updated Soseetha, Sukchai and Agarkar in the rented warehouse.

'A casino,' he told them. 'Pillai is putting in 40 per cent of the money and has pretty much been pouring everything he has into it. The returns, if he pulls it off, will be immense. Looks like we hit them harder than we thought we would with that attack on the massage parlour.'

Agarkar chuckled.

'Good,' he said.

'I take it Shetty is going to be the frontman for this as well?' Sukchai said, and Kaewnan nodded.

Over the fifteen days that he had been working with the three Thai cops, Agarkar had figured out the significance of each member. Sukchai was clearly the one-woman think tank. She could reason, deduce and pick up on things faster than anyone else on the team, and she hardly missed anything. A few days ago, he had given her the call and data records of the private detectives Pillai had hired to get dirt on two of his targets, and he had a feeling she was going to pull off some kind of a miracle with them.

Soseetha, with his burly build and huge ear-to-ear smile, looked like everyone's favourite uncle. Apart from being the technical expert, he had amassed an array of informants in the Bangkok underworld, something that was obvious from the knowledgeable way he spoke during their meetings, and there was also the fact that he had friends in low places who could help him with anything he wanted.

Kaewnan was clearly the leader. He was more

experienced than the other two and was not afraid to take risks if he believed in the objective.

If they had been with the Mumbai Police, Agarkar thought, they'd have racked up the most number of encounters to their name as a team.

'Where are they setting up this casino?' Soseetha asked.

'Silom. They've already bought a property near the Chong Nonski sky train station, an old hotel which they're converting. The plan is to get it up and running within three months. Meesang says the interior is almost done, and supplies have started coming in,' Kaewnan said. 'It's not far from Patpong,' he told Agarkar.

'Once it starts, Pillai is going to be rolling in money and will start buying up officials, including cops. Plus, he'll be Sangsorn's partner, which will pretty much make him untouchable,' Sukchai added.

'I have a question,' Agarkar said, and the three Thai cops turned to him.

'How far are we prepared to go to get Pillai?'

'When you say "we" ...' Kaewnan began, and Agarkar nodded.

'I mean you. As in you and Mr Anantasu. How serious are you about this?'

'Very serious.'

'Serious enough to declare war on Sangsorn?' Agarkar asked. 'Because that's what it'll mean if we hit this casino. Sangsorn has a direct stake in it. There could be repercussions.'

'Not if we play it smart,' Kaewnan said.

'Meaning?'

'I've been thinking of the same thing. Much as I would love it, Sangsorn is not a problem that is going to disappear overnight, and there will be blood on the streets if we go after him.'

Everyone nodded.

'But what if we make it look like it's Pillai's fault? Whatever we do, if Pillai ends up being held responsible for it ...'

'We might not even have to kill him ourselves,' Sukchai said. 'Sangsorn might do it for us.'

'You have a plan?' Agarkar asked.

'I'm working on it. I'll need to talk to the commissioner first.'

'I've got explosives ready and waiting if and when you need them, boss,' Soseetha said.

'Good man,' Kaewnan responded.

'So, what now?' said Agarkar.

'Now,' Kaewnan said, 'we go to my place. My wife's cooking and it is a matter of personal disgrace for me that you haven't had a single home-cooked Thai meal yet.'

18

Shakti Pillai was fidgety.

By this time, he was usually on his third beer, watching a movie or getting a lap dance from one of the many girls that SP arranged for him on a regular basis, not sitting in a dimly lit room in a nightclub.

The evening had started to go wrong for him around two hours ago when SP had walked into his room and given him the bad news. Pillai hadn't even had the time to throw a fit before one of his three phones started ringing. He let it ring twice, finally answering when the caller refused to take the damn hint.

'What?' he barked into the phone.

'Sangsorn would like to see you,' the voice at the other end said. 'Now.'

Pillai and SP made their way to the address they were given. At the door, two burly Thai henchmen escorted Pillai inside, making it clear to SP that he was to wait outside.

After an hour, the door opened and Sangsorn walked in, dressed in a black suit. Floated in, was more like it. The crime lord was thin, with a pinched face that was always smiling in a friendly manner, though his narrow eyes exuded menace. Without saying a word, Sangsorn took a seat opposite Pillai, his eyes staring unblinkingly, the smile fixed on his face.

'Mr Pillai,' he said finally.

'Mr Sangsorn,' Pillai replied.

'Tell me about your cocaine consignment.'

Pillai winced. The man always went straight to business.

'It was supposed to go the usual way. Our man was to pick up the consignment from a parking lot and bring it here.'

'Except he didn't,' Sangsorn said.

'Well, Mr Sangorn, I'm still trying to find out what exactly happened ...'

'Tell me whatever you know.'

Pillai took a deep breath.

'One of our men was supposed to get here with the drugs two nights ago. When he didn't show up, our first thought was that he had run off with the drugs. We kept the supply going. The suppliers weren't worried, and frankly, it was a problem at our end, not theirs.'

'Till today.'

Pillai sighed.

'Tell me about today, Mr Pillai.'

'Well, today, we sent one of our men to a diner on the outskirts of Sukhumvit. It's a little place, tucked out of the way, and we've used its parking lot before.'

Sangsorn only stared.

'The man didn't turn up for three hours. We tried calling him and there was no answer. So we sent someone to the diner.'

'And what did they find?'

Pillai ran a hand through his hair before replying.

'Two cars, side by side, on fire in the parking lot. The first car belonged to our man who had gone missing three days ago. The other belonged to the one we sent today.'

Pillai looked at Sangsorn.

'Go on, Mr Pillai,' the crime lord said.

Pillai hated the way Sangsorn made him feel. The gangster liked to think he was fearless. But this short, thin man, who acted like he was your best friend while his eyes remained cold, was more than he could take.

'The first car had our missing delivery man in the trunk, and the other car had today's runner, as well as the suppliers' man.'

'How did you recognise them?'

'The bodies weren't completely burned when my man got there. He recognised our delivery men, and I spoke to the suppliers an hour later, who confirmed that the third man was theirs.'

'And the drugs?

'They were burned. The fumes were making everyone dizzy.'

There was silence.

Then Sangsorn spoke.

'What happened then?'

Pillai fought the urge to grind his teeth. The bastard was making it worse by forcing him to say it.

'The suppliers called half an hour later. They're suspending supply till we sort this out.'

'And how do we sort it out, Mr Pillai?'

Pillai said nothing.

'Answer me, Mr Pillai. How are we going to sort this out?'

Pillai maintained a stubborn silence.

Sangsorn leaned forward in his chair, his eyes glowing with menace.

'If you have no idea what you're going to do, Mr Pillai, can you at least be a fucking man and admit it?' he asked, each word like a whiplash.

For a moment, the room was silent. Sangsorn slowly leaned back, pulled out a pack of cigarettes from his pocket and lit one. He took a puff and exhaled slowly, the smoke hanging over their heads in a cloud.

'Here's what I want you to understand, Mr Pillai,' he said finally. 'I have taken a chance with you by making you a partner. But that partnership comes with certain responsibilities. Our deal was that you make sure the operations part of our little project goes off without any problems. But now I see that you can't even manage your own establishments.'

'It's not like that—' Pillai began.

'It's not?' Sangsorn lashed out. 'First, your nightclub manager is murdered. Maybe it is a robbery. Maybe it is not. Then, someone goes after your drug supply chain.

And keep in mind, this is a chain I helped you set up, using my goodwill, which counts for something in this city. Normally, one delivery man going missing would have been enough to alarm me. That is how I stay on top. But you ...'

Sangsorn shot Pillai a look of contempt before going on.

'You are too busy giving interviews to news channels and pretending you are on top of the fucking world. And while you're enjoying this fame back in your country, someone strikes your massage parlour. A parlour that, I have to add, used to be under my protection. Do you know who was behind that attack?'

Pillai shook his head. 'Not yet,' he said, reluctant to admit it to Sangsorn.

'Well, then, find out!' Sangsorn snapped. 'It was no one from here. That much I have found out for sure while you were busy enjoying yourself. It must be one of your enemies from back home.'

Pillai was silent.

'I need to make one thing clear, Mr Pillai. At no cost will I tolerate any losses to my own business simply because you cannot clean up your mess. If this—whatever it is that is going on—if it touches a single brick of my casino, I shall withdraw my protection, and that will be after you have reimbursed me for my losses. Do you understand?'

Pillai nodded.

'And I don't want the cash flow from your side to be interrupted. I am honouring my end of our deal to the letter, and I expect the same from you, regardless of what problems you are facing.'

'Yes, Mr Sangsorn.'

Sangsorn threw his half-smoked cigarette on the floor, stood up and walked out.

Pillai sat in the semi-darkness for a good ten minutes, thinking hard, after which he stood up slowly. The nightclub was operating in full swing, and Pillai walked out through the rear exit. He walked around the block and reached his car.

SP, whom he had left sitting in the car, was nowhere to be seen.

✦

Agarkar was laughing so hard he thought he was going to choke. Sukchai and Kaewnan's wife, Potjnat, were shaking with laughter too.

They were sprawled out on couches and easy chairs in Kaewnan's living room. Kaewnan was in the middle of a story.

'I mean, one second I'm exchanging fire with a Turkish drug dealer and the next second our boy here,' he said, pointing at Soseetha, 'comes charging out of the brothel wearing nothing but his underpants, with a gun in each hand. It was the sight of him that distracted the shooters. I was distracted myself. Nearly dropped my gun!'

'I was undercover,' Soseetha said, in an attempt to explain the situation to Agarkar. 'I was doing what I was supposed to do when suddenly I heard gunshots outside. How was I to know Kaewnan was chasing drug peddlers? I thought lives were in danger!'

'Yeah, well, at least you shouldn't have worn pink underpants, Soseetha,' Kaewnan said, and everyone, except Soseetha, howled with laughter.

'*It was part of my disguise*!' Soseetha yelled over the sound of laughter, and everyone burst out laughing again.

It took a good five minutes for order to be restored in the room, after which Agarkar looked at his watch.

'It's late,' he said. 'I should get back to the hotel.'

'Yeah,' Soseetha concurred. 'Been a long day.'

'Thanks for this, Kaewnan. And thank you for a lovely meal, Mrs Kaewnan,' Agarkar said, bowing his head. Kaewnan's wife smiled, while Kaewnan patted Agarkar on the shoulder.

'See you tomorrow, Agarkar,' he said.

Agarkar, Sukchai and Soseetha stepped out of Kaewnan's modest house and walked to where Soseetha and Sukchai had parked their cars.

'I'll drop you,' Sukchai told Agarkar. 'Your hotel's on my way.'

'Thanks,' he said, smiling, and slid into the passenger seat after exchanging a high-five with Soseetha.

It was a cool night and Sukchai drove with the windows down.

'Next time, I'm getting my nephew here. He'll love the place,' Agarkar said.

'Nephew?' Sukchai asked.

'Sister's kid. We're close,' Agarkar said, smiling.

'You don't have any of your own?' she said.

'I'm not married.' Agarkar smiled.

'Oh.'

Agarkar chuckled inwardly. It amused him how people always assumed that if you were past a certain age, you had to be married.

'What about you?' he asked.

'Divorced,' Sukchai said.

It was Agarkar's turn to say 'oh'.

'I'm sorry,' he added.

Sukchai waved her hand dismissively before placing it back on the steering wheel.

'It wasn't much of a marriage anyway,' she said. 'He's a doctor. We both thought we loved each other enough to make it work despite the demands of our respective careers. Then we realised that we didn't. He moved to the Philippines.'

Agarkar nodded. 'I guess that's why I never got married. I never felt sure about anyone,' he mused.

'Better safe than sorry, I guess,' Sukchai responded, and they sat in silence for a while.

'I forgot to ask you,' Agarkar said. 'Did anything come out of those phone records I gave you? The CDRs of the private detectives in Mumbai that Pillai hired ...'

Sukchai lightly slapped her forehead.

'I'm so stupid,' she said. 'Yes, I did find something but I completely forgot about it. I'm so sorry.'

'Don't be,' Agarkar replied. 'A lot's been happening lately.'

'Yes, but this could be important. In fact, I reached out to someone in the Cyber Crime unit for help. His reply is sort of the final piece in the puzzle. He must have sent it by now.'

'Now I'm curious,' Agarkar said.

Sukchai glanced at him.

'Want to come over to my place and take a look? If you're not too tired?'

'Yeah, sure. You seem pretty kicked about it,' Agarkar said.

Sukchai smiled.

'You won't regret it,' she said.

19

'THIS IS … THIS IS the same area where …' she began, looking around, and Khanna nodded without taking his eyes off the road.

It was seven days since her parents had been killed. An hour back, Khanna had called to tell her that he would be picking her up in ten minutes. Now, they were driving down the highway on the outskirts of Delhi and she recognised it as the same area where she had been held captive.

Khanna slowed down and then stopped near the run-down, abandoned structure. They got off and walked through a gate that was hanging by its hinges. When they reached the structure, she saw that the door, which she remembered had been falling apart, had been replaced with a sturdy new one. She was willing to bet this was Khanna's doing.

Khanna took a key from his pocket, unlocked the door, and led her inside. Tied to a chair was a man in his forties. His face was bleeding, he had a black eye and he was gagged with a handkerchief.

'Sit,' Khanna told her, gesturing at a couple of chairs in the room. She took one.

Khanna walked over to the man and removed his gag. 'Tell her what you told me,' he said simply.

The man took a couple of deep breaths before he started speaking.

'I ... I was one of the men who ... who robbed your house that night,' he said to her. 'We were told that your family is very wealthy.'

'By whom?' she asked coldly.

'Shabnam,' the man replied. 'She ... she'd borrowed some money from us and couldn't pay it back. We finally told her that we'd hurt her if she didn't, and she told us about your house. She ... she told us that we could take whatever we wanted on the condition that we let her leave the country. That was the only way she could ensure that we wouldn't bother her for more.'

'Why take me?' she asked.

There was silence.

'Why?' she repeated.

'We ... we have contacts in brothels.'

'You bastard,' she said, standing up. 'You bloody sonofabitch,' she said, walking up to him. 'Which one of you killed my parents?'

'It was the other two. I swear. I was loading some of the stuff in our tempo. When I came to the garage to find the others, there was blood all over the floor and they were standing in it.'

She stepped back, then twisted and delivered a roundhouse kick straight to the man's face. The impact tipped the chair over and he fell back with a crash. She was already through the door when he hit the ground.

Khanna walked out to find her standing near the gate, fists clenched, breathing heavily. Gently, he placed his hands on her shoulders and led her to his car. Then he went back to the shack and, fifteen minutes later, the smell of burning wood reached her nostrils. She turned to see him running out just as the flames started breaking through the walls of the structure.

Wordlessly, he got behind the wheel, turned the key and started driving.

'Did I kill him?' she asked.

'No,' he told her. 'I did.'

She looked at him curiously.

'Who are you?' she asked him.

He kept driving.

An hour later, they were standing on the terrace of her house and she asked him the question again.

'Just someone who can do things a lot of people can't,' he said.

'Abba mentioned once that you were in the army,' she said.

He turned to look at her.

'You're not going to give up, are you?' he asked.

'I learned how not to from the best.' She smiled slightly.

Khanna sighed and leaned against the railing.

'Yes, I was in the army. I'm not going to tell you what I did there. But on one of my missions in foreign territory, your father saved my life.'

He turned to her with fire in his eyes.

'He was one of the most decent men I have ever known. And one of the bravest. There were bullets flying around and he stopped to help me; if not for him, I would have bled to death. He did not deserve to die the way he did. I'm just trying to restore some balance to the world.'

'I want to help,' she said.

He shook his head.

'I can't let you.'

'Well, I'm not asking, am I?' she snapped. 'They were my parents.'

'Look,' he said, turning to her. 'I can completely understand your thirst for revenge. And in a way, I am to blame. If I had not taken you to see that man tonight, you might have sat back and let the law take its course.'

'So why did you?' she asked.

'I don't know.'

'Rubbish!' she said. 'You're not a believer in the law taking its own course. I can tell. And after all that has happened, neither am I. You found one of them before the cops did. You can find the other two as well.'

'I already did,' he said, looking away.

She took a minute to understand.

'You already ...?'

He nodded.

'Their bodies were behind that shack. I kept the third one alive so he could confess to you.'

'Why not the other two?' she said, her voice rising.

'Because you would have wanted to kill them. And I don't want you getting your hands bloody.'

'Well, guess what! I want my hands bloody. And I am going to find that bitch who pretended to be my friend and pulled my world apart, whether you help me or not!' she said before turning away and storming off to her room.

He went after her.

'What're you going to do? Go all the way to Bangkok and—'

He stopped.

She turned around and looked hard at him.

'Where in Bangkok?' she said.

He said nothing.

'Sir, where in Bangkok?'

He stayed silent, looking at her.

'Goddammit, sir, where in Bangkok?'

'I need you to think about this tonight,' he said finally. 'If you still want to do this tomorrow, we'll talk then.'

Before she could say anything, he turned around and left the house.

✦

Venus heard her phone ring and checked the time before answering it.

The call was from a local landline number. She had a fair idea who it was. This was a second cell phone she had activated minutes before emailing Raghav Shetty, and the number had been mentioned in her email.

'Is this Ms Maya Sahani?' a heavily accented female voice asked.

'Yes?'

'Please hold for Mr Raghav Shetty,' the woman said, and Venus smiled.

Venus met Shetty an hour later at the Erawan Tea Room, one of the nine restaurants in the Grand Hyatt Erawan. He came alone, looking a bit haggard despite his crisp suit and carefully combed jet black hair, and Venus couldn't blame him.

After they had ordered Thai tea for her and espresso with milk foam for him, Shetty delicately broached the business at hand.

'Ms Sahani ...' he began.

'The investment opportunity,' she said, smiling at him. She had pulled her hair back in a bun and was wearing a business suit. She looked completely different from the ponytailed, t-shirt-and-jeans-sporting photographer that she had been playing. Only a close observer would recognise her, and that too, only if they had seen her before.

'Yes,' he said, nodding and smiling back at her. 'You see, I'm curious as to why you approached me.'

'Well, I did some discreet research before coming to Bangkok, and am obviously more comfortable starting an alliance with a fellow Indian. I am told you're setting up a casino here, and I thought this would be a good chance for me to see my money grow. This is a tourist hub, after all.'

'Yes, well, I must be upfront with you. One of my other establishments recently suffered something of a setback. You might have seen the news about a massage parlour being attacked?'

'That was yours?' she asked with perfectly feigned concern.

He nodded.

'You would have found out eventually, and I did not want to be dishonest. But I also assure you that the casino is in a different location, away from the areas prone to gang-related violence. It is much better protected, both as an establishment and an investment.'

'I would like to see the site before we go ahead,' she said.

'That can easily be arranged. If I might ask, what kind of investment did you have in mind?'

'Oh, something like ten to fifteen crore rupees,' she said. 'For a casino, the returns would be really high, wouldn't they?'

The waiter arrived with their orders and Shetty took the chance to do the math in his head. Fifteen crore rupees was more than a hundred million Thai baht. With that kind of money, and the cash that Pillai was already raising, things would get a lot easier.

'The returns,' he told her, 'would be unimaginable. When would you like to see the site?'

'Now?' she asked.

'Why delay auspicious work, right?' he asked, smiling. 'It's ten minutes away, Ms Sahani.'

Venus smiled back at him. 'Please. Call me Maya.'

As they got into Shetty's car, Agarkar stepped on the accelerator and overtook them.

The team had decided that it was best if Agarkar took care of the surveillance on Shetty because he could blend in by posing as a tourist. Agarkar was also hoping to be able to eavesdrop on a conversation or two. Soseetha had promised to arrange for a couple of long-range parabolic microphones to help with the eavesdropping, and Agarkar had no reason to doubt that the big man would get anything but the best.

In the back seat, Sultan Aziz, secure behind tinted windows, took a series of photographs using a professional camera equipped with a telephoto lens.

'Transfer them to the laptop and email them to Kaewnan,' Agarkar told him, looking at the rear view mirror before slowing down and letting Shetty's car pass. He smoothly fell in behind it and drove slowly, making sure there was enough distance between the two vehicles. Halfway into the journey, he had a fair idea of where they were going.

'I think they're going to the casino,' he said. 'Tell Kaewnan.'

Sultan didn't reply. He was too busy staring at the laptop he was holding.

'Sultan?' Agarkar said sharply.

He looked up and met Agarkar's eyes in the rear view mirror.

'What?' Agarkar asked.

'That woman with him,' Sultan said, and Agarkar could almost see his brain working furiously. 'I'm not sure, but ... but I think I know her.'

20

WAJID QURESHI'S HOUSE was located in one of those many little lanes in Dongri that you would never find if you went by the postal address.

As with a lot of localities in Mumbai, places were found with the help of locals—a shopkeeper who delivered something to the house you were looking for, or a barber who happened to know the man you were trying to find.

On that afternoon in Dongri, two weeks after Agarkar landed in Bangkok, a man carrying a briefcase stopped at a grocery shop to ask the same question for the third time.

'Do you know the way to Wajid bhai's house?'

The shopkeeper looked up from his ledger.

'Which one, my friend?' he said.

'Wajid Qureshi,' the man replied. 'The one who has an office in Musafirkhana?'

The shopkeeper's smile was wide.

'Of course I know him, bhaisahab. That building right in front of my humble little shop is where our Wajid Qureshi stays. You're a friend?'

The question could have elicited a 'none of your business' anywhere else. But not here. Shopkeepers in such localities considered it their right to know everything that was going on in every household.

The man gave a small smile.

'Just a business associate,' he said before turning away.

On a stool placed just outside the grocery shop, a heavyset man lowered the newspaper he was reading and stared at the outsider. As he walked towards Wajid Qureshi's building, the heavyset man stood up, placed the newspaper on the stool, and started following him.

On the first floor, the heavyset man caught up with the man carrying the briefcase and tapped him on the shoulder.

'My name is Sohail,' he said. 'I work for Wajid bhai. Who are you?'

'Jigar Patel,' the man said. 'I was called here by Wajid bhai.'

Sohail nodded and took Patel to the second floor landing where he subjected Patel to a body search. Then he led Patel to one of the doors, on which he knocked discreetly. It opened a crack first, and the eyes beyond it peered for a moment. Sohail nodded and the door opened wider. The three men in the living room acknowledged Sohail as he entered with Patel.

Sohail led Patel to the inner room where Wajid and two other men were counting cash.

Wajid looked up at Patel with surprise.

'*Kya* Patel?' he asked. '*Idhar kaise?*'

There was silence in the room for half a minute.

'You ... you asked me to come meet you,' Patel said, confused.

Wajid put the money that he was holding on the table in front of him.

'Me?' he asked.

'Wajid bhai, you called me an hour ago. I went to your office in Musafirkhana and they told me you were here. They said to come here and ask for—'

At that instant, gunshots exploded outside the house and the door fell apart. The three guards in the living room sprang to their feet but were cut down under the hail of shots from fully automatic submachine pistols. The assailants, four in number, went straight for the inner room where Wajid was making a mad scramble for his gun, which lay on a nearby table.

The four assailants smiled. The problem wasn't speed, they had been told. What would work in their favour was that Wajid Qureshi, one of Maqsood Alam's top lieutenants in Mumbai, would be overconfident. Thanks to years of enjoying the power that came with running Maqsood's extortion racket in the city, it had not crossed Wajid's mind that someone could attack him in his own house.

Sohail and the other two men in the room brought their guns up just as the bullets from their attackers' guns reached them. They, too, had been slowed down by their smug overconfidence, and had wasted the crucial first few seconds of the attack staring wide-eyed and slack-jawed.

All the three went down to the bullets, while the leader of the attackers went over to Wajid and put a gun to his head.

'Do you know who my boss is, you motherfucker?' Wajid asked through clenched teeth.

The lead gunman reached behind him and felt around the table full of cash till he found Wajid's cell phone.

'Call him,' the gunman said, handing him the phone. 'Now.'

With shaking hands, Qureshi dialled a number from memory. After the fifth ring, the call was answered.

'Bhai … Wajid …' was all Qureshi could say before the gunman snatched the phone away.

'Haan, tell me,' Shabbir Khan said from the other end.

'Listen,' the gunman said, and pulled the trigger. 'Shakti Pillai says salaam,' he added before hanging up and tossing the phone away.

As he looked up from the couch where Wajid lay, his head a mess of blood and brain, he saw Patel, who had run behind the couch at the first sound of gunfire, slowly get up, his hands shaking like leaves, sweat flowing down his face in rivulets.

The leader smiled.

'Just so you know,' he said, 'it was me who called you.'

Patel opened his mouth to speak but no sound came out. The gunman raised his weapon and shot a burst of automatic fire into Patel's face.

Unslinging a satchel that he had around his shoulder, he pulled out a two-litre canister of petrol. His three men moved to the living room while he poured half of it on the floor.

All of them threw down their guns and ammunition. The leader emptied the rest of the petrol on the living room floor, ignited a matchstick and threw it into the bedroom.

The fire spread quickly and the four men ran out. At the same time, the flames shot out of the windows, leading to cries of 'Fire!' from the street below and bringing other residents out of their houses.

The four gunmen threw themselves into the throng of screaming men and women squeezing into the narrow staircase.

Four patrolling constables, who had rushed to the building after hearing the sound of gunfire while passing by, were physically pushed back by the mob. One of the gunmen even caught a constable who was falling to the ground before running by him into the street.

✦

The joint commissioner of police, Satish Kulkarni, was fuming.

The IPS officer was the head of the Mumbai Crime Branch, and he liked to think he was doing a damn fine job of it.

Over the last one year of his posting, he had worked hard to make sure that peace prevailed on the streets of the city. Like many officers before him—and like many would after him—he had established a tacit understanding with the underworld. The underworld would never be truly finished, no matter what the politicians liked to say. It was their job to shoot their mouths off, and it was the police's job to make sure that the underworld stayed within its limits.

Which is why crimes like extortion, in which the crooked on the wrong side of the law took money from the crooked on the right side, were tolerated.

What was not tolerated, Kulkarni thought furiously, was a bloodbath in the middle of a densely populated residential area, followed by a fire that resulted in a near stampede that left seven innocent people injured, two of them seriously.

What was also not tolerated, he thought, tightening his palm around a paperweight, was the murder of one of the richest garments exporters in the city. That the businessman, Patel, was one of the biggest financiers of the Maqsood Alam gang was a different matter. He was also the man who had posed for photographs with everyone from the chief minister downwards. Sure, he supplied money by the crores to the gang, but he also kept his hands largely clean and had friends in high places.

Which was why his murder was going to bring a lot of unwanted flak to the police department in general and the Crime Branch in particular.

'Play it again,' Kulkarni told Police Inspector Hemant Sathe, who headed the Anti Extortion Cell.

At Kulkarni's instructions, Sathe had put Wajid's cell phone under surveillance. When the killers made Wajid call Shabbir, Sathe's team had picked it up. In fact, that was how Sathe, and subsequently Kulkarni, learned about the shootout in the first place, because the veteran cop listening in on Wajid's phone knew a gunshot when he heard one.

'Bhai … Wajid …'

'Haan, bolo.'

'Suno.'

Boom boom boom.

'Shakti Pillai says salaam.'

'Automatic?' Kulkarni asked.

Sathe nodded.

'We're thinking submachine guns. Forensic guys are still going through what's left of the house. I've asked them to look for shells.'

Kulkarni was silent for a while.

'I want the bastards who did this,' he said finally.

'We're working on it, sir.'

'Work harder. I have a pissed off commissioner to answer to,' Kulkarni said before dismissing his subordinate.

Five minutes later, Kulkarni picked up one of the four cell phones in his desk drawer and dialled a number.

'Tell Pillai to get in touch,' he said to the man at the other end before disconnecting.

✦

The email from Amarchand Mehra was brief but firm.

'Please call asap,' it said.

After accepting the contract on Pillai, Venus had given Mehra an email ID through which he could stay in touch.

Now she opened up an internet calling programme on her cell phone and used a Bluetooth wireless earpiece to talk as she went around the warehouse that Hammer had rented for her, preparing for the next step in her plan.

'It's me,' she said as the call connected.

'You heard what happened here?' Mehra asked.

Venus had. The news alerts system she had set up was doing its work. Two hours after the shootout in Dongri, she had begun receiving alerts about it, including an interview Pillai had given, this time to a different news channel.

'Arrey, all of them were Maqsood Alam's dogs,' he said. 'I've done the cops a favour by cleaning up that corner of Dongri.'

'What about Mr Jigar Patel?' the reporter asked.

'What about him? You think he was some innocent man caught in the gunfire? What was he doing in Wajid Qureshi's house then?'

'He does not have a criminal record.'

'Yaar, you are so naive. Okay, I have to go now. I'll be in touch,' Pillai said before hanging up.

Venus replied to Mehra's question in the affirmative. There was a moment's silence.

'Is there something I should know?' she asked.

'Jigar Patel was one of us,' Mehra said. 'I mean, one of the eight who pooled in to pay you for your … services.'

'How much did he pool in?' she asked.

'A hundred crore. Same as the rest of us.'

'I'm transferring a hundred crore to your account. Please make sure it reaches his family.'

'It's not the money we're worried about Ms … Venus,' Mehra said.

'I know. Consider it a gesture of good faith. Also, know that I have not exactly been idle all this while. I won't tell you the details because the less you know, the better, but I can tell you that I am ready to make my final move. You'll hear from me in a few days.'

'I hope so. Good luck.'

Mehra ended the call.

Venus went back to packing.

21

THE BOARD IN the warehouse rented by Kaewnan had a new picture pinned to it. This one was not positioned next to Pillai and SP's photographs. It was some distance away from all of them.

'Saba Mansoor,' Kaewnan said, looking at Agarkar, Sukchai and Soseetha. 'That is the name on her passport. She landed at Suvarnabhumi twenty-one days ago, which is three days before you did, Agarkar.'

The Indian cop nodded and Kaewnan went on.

'Agarkar and Aziz saw her while tailing Shetty. She met him at the Grand Hyatt Erawan yesterday. They arrived separately but left together. Agarkar?'

Agarkar stood up.

'Sultan recognised her because he had met her at Pillai's nightclub the same night that we ... recruited him ...' there were chuckles, '... into our little team. He spoke to her at length and even gave her his number. Now, we don't know what she was doing with Shetty and we don't know if her visit to his nightclub was just a coincidence. So, we set about investigating her.'

The three cops were listening attentively.

'Sultan and I followed them to the site of the casino, where they spent a good hour before leaving. If Shetty offered to drop her somewhere, she declined and took a cab. This is where it got interesting.'

Everyone leaned forward a bit.

'Well, she got off on Rama III Road and walked for five minutes. During this time, she crossed the street twice, clearly checking for a tail. The first time she did, I drove past her and pulled over, pretending to talk on my phone. She passed by me and took a quick look at me while walking by. I could not risk her recognising me, so I turned around to come here.'

'But?' Sukchai asked.

'But I had seen two security cameras on the road, and I immediately informed Kaewnan. He spoke to the local police station, who started tracking her movements through the camera network.'

'We got lucky,' Kaewnan said. 'A camera caught her entering a small warehouse, much smaller than ours. The local police kept an eye on the feed till she came back out. And when she did, she looked completely different. Her hair was different. Her clothes were different. And she had a backpack. She hailed another taxi from there. The camera caught the number and we tracked down the driver. He told us he dropped her at a hotel in Thonburi.'

'Must've been easy after that,' Soseetha said.

Agarkar and Kaewnan both nodded.

'I went to the hotel and asked to check their guest records as a routine check. Took down details of ten guests from different countries, including our woman. Saba Mansoor. Passport says she is from New Delhi,' Kaewnan said.

'And listen to this,' Agarkar said. 'The Delhi Police sent a team to the address mentioned in her passport. 'It turned out to be a restaurant.'

Soseetha and Sukchai straightened.

'Bogus passport?' Soseetha asked.

'Looks like it. But the point is that, apart from her address not being what it is, she was seen in our target's nightclub, then in his company and also seems to be trained in detecting a tail. All of that put together is not something we can ignore. My chief back in Mumbai is working on finding out more about this woman. Meanwhile, we need to watch her.'

'Why not just pick her up right now for the bogus passport?' Soseetha asked.

'It won't tell us why she's trying to get close to our target. There is no guarantee she will break down and start telling us what we want to know. All she has to do is get a lawyer, who will whisk her back to India,' Sukchai said.

'I have a team watching the hotel right now. If she leaves, we'll know about it. Another team is outside Shetty's house, while a third is watching the casino site. Right now, we're back to wait and watch,' Kaewnan added.

'Not necessarily,' Agarkar said, smiling at Sukchai. 'Right?' he added, and she blushed a little as she stood up.

Kaewnan looked at her curiously. 'Still shy about taking the stage, eh, Sukchai?' he said, and her cheeks went a shade darker as she came up to the board.

'So, Agarkar gave me the CDRs of the private detectives used by Pillai's gang. Two of Pillai's targets are having extramarital affairs, while the third is a closet gay. Pillai exposed one of the two adulterers, and the other two got so scared that they continue to pay him every month to this day. Did I get that right?' she directed the last question at Agarkar, who nodded.

Sukchai continued, 'So I checked all calls made and received by these detectives. For each detective, I found one cell phone number that is no longer active. Each of these numbers was in touch with the respective private eye for around three months, which is, in theory, enough time to tail a man and get evidence of his sins. We agree?'

They all nodded.

'So, I then asked Agarkar for CDRs of these three numbers, which he obtained and gave me earlier this week. It was these that I was analysing for several days, and I only pieced it together the night we came over to your place for dinner, Kaewnan.'

Kaewnan nodded, clearly curious about what was to come.

'So, say I email you something using my phone and you reply to me. My IP address and yours will show in the CDRs. That is how we track exchange of data using mobile internet.'

'Are you telling me you found Pillai's IP address?' Sosetha asked excitedly.

Sukchai shrugged.

'I don't know,' she said. 'But there's only one Bangkok-based IP address in all the CDRs. One of the three now-defunct numbers exchanged some internet data with this IP address around two months ago. I only learned the other night that the IP was Bangkok-based. And we are now tracking it.'

Kaewnan stood up, looking as excited as Soseetha.

'Where is it now?' he asked. 'What's the location?'

Sukchai made a face.

'We can't find it,' she said.

There was a minute's silence.

Then Agarkar spoke.

'What she means is that it cannot be tracked right now because it is not online. Possibly because its cellular internet is not on.'

Sukchai nodded.

'The moment it gets switched on, we will know,' she said.

'This is good, Sukchai,' Kaewnan said. 'This is really good.'

Soseetha came over to bump fists with her while Agarkar stood leaning against one of the tables, smiling at her.

As Kaewnan stepped out to get some fresh air and Soseetha left to fetch food for them, Sukchai and Agarkar found themselves alone in the warehouse.

Agarkar walked over to where Sukchai was standing, her back to him, looking at the pictures on the board. It had been empty when Agarkar first entered the place. Now it was full of pictures, including mugshots of the key players, and surveillance photographs.

Hesitantly, Agarkar raised his hands and put them on Sukchai's shoulders. She leaned back into him and he wrapped his arms around her waist.

'You want to come over tonight?' she asked, letting him nuzzle his face into her neck.

'Oh yes, please,' he whispered into her neck, and they both smiled.

✦

In a plush villa in Bangkok, Shakti Pillai took a gulp of his fifth chilled beer and let out a contented sigh.

Things had been looking bad for him for a while, what with the problems with his massage parlour and the drug supply to his nightclub.

The biggest blow he had taken was the loss of his lieutenant, or so he thought.

After he had failed to find SP in his car, he had found a pay phone and called SP's number. It was answered by a nurse who said she was speaking to him from the Bangkok Christian Hospital, not far from Patpong.

Pillai had rushed there to find SP unconscious, an array of tubes sticking out of him. He was bandaged in several places, including his head.

'What happened?' he asked.

'He fell down some stairs,' the nurse answered. 'His neighbour brought him in a while ago.'

'Neighbour?' Pillai asked.

The nurse looked around till she found him.

'Over there,' she said.

Pillai turned and found himself looking at one of Sangsorn's bouncers, who smiled at him.

Pillai took another swig of his beer and put the memory out of his mind. This was a time for celebration, he thought. SP was out of danger and he had made arrangements for all expenses to be taken care of.

As he had done some seven times already that day, he marvelled at the smoothness with which the job in Dongri had gone down.

SP worried too much, he thought. And he nagged too much. Had he not been in hospital, he would have probably nagged the hell out of him over the plan to kill Wajid.

SP was over-cautious. He, Pillai, wasn't. He believed in action over thought. He had simply issued the order to use Patel to get to Wajid, and his men in India had done it.

He was already seeing the results. The hit on Wajid had sent out a message that he was not afraid of anyone, not even Maqsood. And Patel's murder had scared a lot of businessmen into paying up, and money had already started coming in, fast.

Plus, Shetty was telling him that the woman who had contacted him was willing to pour something like a hundred million baht into their casino. With all the money combined, Pillai was going to be more than comfortable. The inflow of money would shut up Sangsorn. Then, without the distraction of Sangsorn, he could get down to finding out who was causing all these problems for him.

And then there was the little bonus. The phone call he had received from India an hour ago. At first, he thought it was some kind of a joke. But it wasn't. At least, it didn't seem to be. If the offer he had received worked out, he would never have to worry about anything again. Maqsood would fade away and be forgotten. The police would be left with egg on their faces. And he, Shakti Pillai, would become one of the biggest names in the underworld.

He would take care of this job just as he had the Dongri hit, Pillai decided. No long-drawn discussions with SP, and no compromise. This had to be brazen. It had to be a statement.

Which reminded him of something. Around four hours after the attack in Dongri, one of his men in India had called. Joint Commissioner Kulkarni wanted to speak to him. His man had given him a number that Kulkarni could be reached at.

He had spoken to Kulkarni in the past. Like all gangsters, he had periodic conversations with policemen just to get a sense of which way the wind was blowing.

Kulkarni had made his displeasure about Pillai's growing audaciousness known several times in the past.

Pillai was guessing that Kulkarni would have a lot to say to him this time as well. *Good*, he thought, smiling; he had some things to say to Kulkarni as well.

22

'WHAT DID YOU DO?' she asked Khanna. 'Tell me!'

They were standing at one end of the Khlong Lat Mayom floating market in Bangkok, one of the biggest and busiest markets built over the canals that once used to be the main mode of transport in the city.

The air was thick with the aroma of grilled seafood, meat and vegetables, along with the scent of what seemed like hundreds of different spices. Tourists of all nationalities thronged the market, while natives shopped from boats laden with fruits and vegetables.

'I did what had to be done,' he said, looking away.

'Okay, can you stop acting like I'm a child for five minutes? You do know what I'm here to do?'

Khanna sighed.

'Before I met you, before your father hired me, I was involved with a group of really bad people. I mean, I've done some bad things in my life, but these guys were too much for me as well.'

'Why were you with them then?'

'I owed them. Debts like those take a long time to pay off. Once I did, I came to India. Your father had given me his number and I got in touch. He asked me to come train you. I happily agreed.'

'And these are the guys you had to turn to?' she asked.

'They know a lot of people in a lot of places. If anyone could help me find the whereabouts of a newly migrated Indian woman, it had to be them,' Khanna said as he turned to avoid bumping into a man who was carrying a large plate filled with grilled shrimp.

'Is that why you said that this might be the last time we see each other?' she asked, her heart sinking.

'I owe them now. I have to be ready to do whatever they need me to do.'

'And if you don't?'

'They'll find me. Which is fine. But these people have a way of hitting you where it hurts the most. And I can't let them hurt you in order to get to me.'

She reached out and put her hand in his. He squeezed it tightly.

Then, he said, 'It's here.'

Around a hundred metres from them, a brightly coloured tourist boat full of people came to a stop. The boat offered an hour-long ride through the market, with one stop at a small village in the middle of the canals.

After getting Shabnam's address, she and Khanna had spotted her just as she was leaving her hotel. They had been following her since morning, and it was close to afternoon now.

She was the tenth person to get off the boat. She was dressed in a bright yellow dress, white shoes and a white hat, a stark contrast to the conservative salwar kameez she had always worn during their Urdu sessions.

As she walked through the pier, they discreetly fell into step behind her. Khanna broke off as they exited the market and went to get their car, while her former student stayed on Shabnam's trail, mingling easily with the crowd.

Just as Shabnam was going to step aboard the minibus that was taking the tourists across the city, she drew up alongside her former teacher.

'Salaam, didi,' she said, wrapping an arm around her waist.

Shabnam froze. Gently, her student led her to where Khanna was waiting in his car, and they both got into the back seat.

'Surprise, eh?' was all Khanna said, before turning around and starting the car.

Before Shabnam could say anything, she spoke.

'Ishrat-e-qatra hai dariya mein fanaa ho jaana;

Dard ka hadh se guzarna hai dawaa ho jaaana.'

Shabnam said nothing.

'You know, for a long time, I really didn't know what Ghalib was talking about. You'd always try to explain to me how pain can become so intense that it can turn itself into the cure.'

She turned to look at Shabnam.

'Now I know,' she whispered.

'Gudiya ...' Shabnam began, and her hand shot out, clutching Shabnam's jaw.

'Do not ever call me by that name,' she hissed. 'Pet names are for loved ones.'

'But … but I …'

'Shut up!'

Shabnam flinched as if she'd been slapped.

They drove the rest of the way in silence till they reached her hotel in Pattaya.

'Get out. Let's go to your room,' said Khanna. 'You do anything stupid, I'll strangle you on the spot.'

Shabnam trembled visibly and stiffly got out of the car.

They followed her to the reception desk, where she reclaimed her key, and then up to the second floor. She did not say a word and neither did they.

They entered her suite, and she went over to a table bearing a jug of water and glasses. With trembling hands, she poured herself one as Khanna stationed himself by the door.

Shabnam took a long sip of water and then turned around.

She stared back hard. 'Let's get it over with,' she said coldly.

'Wh … what?' Shabnam asked.

'Your apologies, your explanations, your justifications. Let's get them out of the way.'

Shabnam pulled up a chair and sat down. She looked at the ground for a minute and then looked up.

'I am a survivor,' Shabnam said. 'My father left me with nothing but lakhs of rupees in debt. He killed himself when he couldn't repay the money. I am not like him. I did what I had to do to survive.'

'So that's it, huh? My parents were bludgeoned to death with a hammer, you bitch! Can you imagine that happening to you? Those men were going to sell me to a brothel!'

'You didn't just pay off the debt, did you?' Khanna said. 'From the looks of it, you seem to have helped yourself to some of the money too.'

Shabnam looked down at the floor.

'I'd like to pray one last time,' she said finally.

'Make it fast,' she said harshly, turning to go sit on the bed.

At that instant, the door to the suite opened and a Thai man in his forties entered, a bouquet in his hand and a smile on his face. Both fell within seconds as he took in the tableau before him. The bouquet crashed to the ground and was replaced by a gun so fast that only Khanna's trained eye saw it.

'DOWN!' Khanna roared, and she obeyed on instinct, throwing herself to the floor.

The room reverberated with the sound of gunshots as the Thai man fired three rounds at the exact spot where her back would have been. Khanna launched himself at him and connected with his midriff. They both crashed to the floor and the gun clattered to the ground.

The Thai man was half-sitting when Khanna rolled around and came up behind him, gripping his neck in a stranglehold and twisting hard. Everyone in the room heard the man's neck snap.

Shabnam screamed and went over to him as Khanna stood up, wiping the sweat from his forehead. With tearful eyes, Shabnam looked at Khanna and was about to say something when she felt a cold presence against her head.

She turned around and found herself staring at the barrel of the gun that her Thai friend had dropped in the melee.

'Alvida,' was all Shabnam's former student said as she pulled the trigger. Then everything was silent.

Khanna quickly kicked the door shut and went over to his protégé. He put his hands on her shoulders and led her to the bed and made her sit down. She was still clutching the gun with both her hands when the knocking on the door began.

'Is everything all right, madam?' a man asked in English. 'Please open the door. Are you okay? Are you hurt?'

Five minutes later, security guards kicked in the door. Khanna was on one side of the doorway while she was on the other. Three guards came rushing in and looked around the room. She raised the gun and fired a round in the air, sending the guards, as well as the staff gathered outside, cowering to the floor. They jumped over the crouching forms and ran to the staircase.

Two guards came running up the stairs but Khanna didn't break his stride even as he knocked both of them out.

They ran into the lobby where more guards, stationed on the manager's instructions, came charging towards them. She raised the gun again and pulled the trigger. There was only an empty click. Within seconds, they were surrounded by seven guards.

Master and protégé exchanged a glance before they moved. She threw the gun at one of the guard's heads and he went down without a sound. She grabbed a second guard by his throat while delivering a well-aimed kick in the solar plexus to a third. Behind her, Khanna punched a guard straight in his throat, elbowed another in the nose and took out a third with a kick to his knee.

Two guards remained standing, arms raised defiantly in fighting stances. The one close to her stepped forward. She batted his hands away and drove her palm into his nose, crushing it. He fell to the ground like a dead tree just as Khanna delivered an upper cut to the remaining guard's jaw.

They stood over the fallen guards for a second. Then, Khanna grabbed her hand and they ran towards his car. Two more guards blocked their way. Khanna kicked one in his chest and he fell over backwards, hitting his head on the pavement. The other made a lunge for her and she twirled around to deliver a roundhouse kick. It was meant for his chest but ended up hitting his throat. She actually felt his larynx shatter under her foot.

They slid into the car at almost the same instant and Khanna sped away with a screech of burning rubber.

Within hours, they were both fugitives, wanted for the murder of one Indian citizen, one Thai man with a criminal record, and three Thai security guards, as well as for the attempted murder of several others. The RTP printed out their pictures based on CCTV camera footage of the hotel and released them to the media, while airports, too, were notified.

'Well, you didn't tell me you were going to start a fucking war in there, did you?' Dylan Murphy, Khanna's contact, said to him twenty-four hours later. They were lying low in a cheap hotel in Patpong.

'We didn't know she already had a boyfriend, okay, Murphy?' Khanna said.

'Yeah, where did that guy even come from? Bloody smart move, eh, getting herself a local thug as a minder?' Murphy said.

Khanna shrugged.

'Look, we need help, okay? Tell me what it'll cost us. I'll take care of it.'

'We'll take care of it,' she interjected, and Khanna eyed her dangerously before turning back to Murphy.

'Don't listen to her,' he said.

'I don't know, Khanna,' Murphy said, looking at her with a half-smile on his lips. 'From what I hear, she was pretty good in there. You trained her well, didn't you?'

'Murphy …' Khanna said. 'She's a child. Have a fucking heart.'

'No can do. You don't survive in my world by having a heart. And I ain't running a day care programme here.

I can smuggle you two out, but it's going to cost you both. And it isn't money I need.'

Khanna stepped forward but she put a hand on his arm.

'What's it going to cost us?' she asked.

Khanna turned to stare murderously at her but she ignored him.

'Ever been to Cyprus?' Murphy asked.

✦

Venus lit a cigarette. Every time she came to Bangkok, she would come to the floating market and stare at it, reliving the day she first took a human life.

After fleeing Bangkok, they had spent a year in Cyprus before moving to Syria, and then to Egypt. For five blood-soaked years, they had toured the Middle East, leaving dead bodies in their wake, paying off the debt of the bad people who had done them a good turn.

When the debt was finally paid off, the accent wasn't the only thing that she took away from the Middle East.

23

AGARKAR WOKE UP quite suddenly, but he had always been a restless sleeper. Turning in bed, he found his cell phone and checked the time. It was 2 a.m., which meant it was only 12.30 a.m. back home.

The glow of his cell phone's display caused Sukchai to twitch in her sleep and he quickly put his phone away. Turning, he took a moment to gaze at her in the light of the night lamp. Her jet black hair was splayed across her face and shoulders, and Agarkar resisted the impulse to move it off her face.

After dinner at Kaewnan's place three night ago, Agarkar and Sukchai had come to her place to go over her findings with the CDRs. Sukchai had opened a bottle of wine and, over a glass each, they had gone over her progress.

At her behest, he called up Mathur and requested him to arrange for the CDRs of the three suspects' numbers that she had identified. Sukchai was excited, and refilled their glasses.

'I didn't think this would go anywhere, but it seems to be doing just that,' she said happily.

'Honestly, I didn't know if it would go anywhere either, but I was curious to see what you would do with the data. Kaewnan says you're one of the best he's worked with,' Agarkar said, and Sukchai blushed a little.

'Kaewnan is blindly affectionate towards the people he believes in. He'll praise anyone to the heavens if he likes them.'

'In this case,' Agarkar said, looking into her eyes, 'he was clearly right.'

Sukchai looked away shyly and then steered the conversation back to the CDRs.

For the next one hour, they talked animatedly about technical investigation methods in their respective countries and the challenges they faced. At some point, they moved from her work table to her couch. When she returned after refilling their glasses for the third time, she suggested they stop talking shop. He agreed, and Sukchai put on a movie on her laptop about a former soldier-turned-assassin who walked with a limp after getting injured in the line of duty. The film had English subtitles, and Sukchai explained the cultural references to Agarkar as they watched it.

Neither of them realised when it had happened, but by the end of the movie, Agarkar was spread out on the couch with his head in Sukchai's lap, while she had one hand in his hair and the other on his chest.

Later, they would try to reason with themselves that they were on a high after Sukchai's brilliant work with the CDRs, that they'd had too much wine to drink, that they were both lonely ... But after that night of tender lovemaking, just before Agarkar was leaving for his hotel, he stopped at the door and took Sukchai in his arms.

'I don't want this to be a one-off thing,' he told her.

She raised herself on her toes and kissed him on the lips.

'Neither do I,' she said.

Since then, Agarkar had spent every night with her.

Now, three nights later, Agarkar silently slipped out of the bed and walked over to where his clothes were lying on the floor. Picking up his trousers, he found his pack of cigarettes and lighter and went over to the window of Sukchai's apartment, where he lit one and stared out into the distance.

Halfway through, he felt a presence behind him. He half-turned and put his arm around her. He saw that she had on only an oversized t-shirt.

'What are you thinking about?' she asked him.

He shook his head.

'You'll think it's funny,' he said.

'Tell me anyway.'

'My father,' Agarkar said, taking a drag of his cigarette. 'Nights like these remind me of him. When I was a kid, we'd put out cots outside our house at night and lie down side by side, looking at the stars. He'd talk about his plans to help farmers in the district and I'd tell him about my day at school. I hated the rains because they robbed me of this time with him.'

Sukchai slipped her arm around his waist, drawing him closer.

'Is he …?' she asked.

'No, he's very much alive. It's just that …' Agarkar paused.

Sukchai turned to face him, stroking his chin with her thumb.

'You don't have to tell me if you don't want to,' she said.

Agarkar sighed and ground out his cigarette against the window sill before flicking it out into the street.

'Well, as the number of my encounters grew, so did the number of departmental inquiries against me. My father is a very honest man. Too honest, in my opinion. He couldn't stomach the fact that his son was being investigated. As the media trial mounted, things began to worsen between us. Then, I was accused of corruption and dismissed from service. The day the dismissal was made official, he called me up and told me that he didn't have a son anymore.'

Sukchai said nothing. Agarkar stared out of the window.

'I've done a lot of things in my career which people might not approve of. I knew I was taking risks and I knew a lot of people wouldn't understand my choices. But I never expected my father to react that way. I guess I should have.'

'Is that why you're here?' Sukchai asked him.

'I'm here because Shakti Pillai is truly a piece of

shit and needs to be put down. My father wouldn't understand, but I know it has to be done.'

Sukchai put both her arms around his midriff and hugged him tightly, pressing her cheek against his chest. He brought his other arm up and enveloped her in an embrace, resting his chin on her head.

'You know,' she said, still hugging him, 'I like the way you smell.'

He ran his hand down her back and slipped it under her t-shirt, feeling the smoothness of her skin.

As she snuggled against him, there was a loud, insistent buzz from near the bed.

'That's mine,' Agarkar said, giving her a quick kiss before breaking the embrace to answer his cell phone.

'How soon can you leave your hotel?' Kaewnan asked from the other end.

'Ten, fifteen minutes at the most. What's the matter?'

'Saba Mansoor just left her hotel in Thonburi and is on her way to Rama III Road,' Kaewnan said. 'That warehouse she'd gone to the other day?'

'Oh, right,' Agarkar said, placing the area. 'Where do you want me to meet you?

'Just be ready,' Kaewnan said. 'I'm calling in everyone. I'll send someone to pick you up.'

'If you're calling in everyone,' Agarkar said, 'Sukchai could pick me up. She doesn't stay far away—she dropped me on her way home the other day.'

'Perfect,' Kaewnan said.

Agarkar ended the call and looked at Sukchai.

'Expect a call from Kaewnan,' he told her. 'I'm going to shower.'

✦

Bakshi liked Kodaikanal in the winter. The days were warm and the nights were perfect for a stiff Scotch and soda.

Across the table from him, his friend and former colleague, Sohan Kamat, felt the same way.

'To old times,' Kamat said.

Bakshi raised his own glass and clinked it with Kamat's.

'To old times,' he echoed.

Both men took a sip of their drinks. They were sitting in a rented cottage in Kodaikanal where Kamat was, officially, holidaying. A veteran of the Research and Analysis Wing, Kamat was known for being a workaholic. The running joke was that if Kamat was on holiday, it was to ensure that someone somewhere was having a really bad day.

When Bakshi had called Kamat two days ago, the latter had told him he was 'on holiday', which Bakshi understood to mean that he was heading some operation or the other. Bakshi told Kamat that he was needed and added that he would come down to Kodaikanal to meet him.

'And new times too?' Kamat asked, looking at Bakshi over the rim of his glass.

Bakshi had to chuckle.

The two men had first crossed paths when Bakshi was posted with the IB, shortly after his promotion to deputy inspector general fifteen years ago. Kamat, a career intelligence man, was a young SP and had already been with RAW for three years when Bakshi first met him. Over the five years that Bakshi worked on deputation with the IB, he had several opportunities to work with Kamat, and the two men had developed a mutual affection. They stayed in touch after Bakshi's deputation was complete, and Kamat would pass on the occasional nugget of information to Bakshi while he was serving, and Bakshi would return the favour by unofficially helping Kamat out whenever he or his men needed anything in Mumbai.

'What are you implying, Kamat?' Bakshi asked, grinning slightly.

'Oh, nothing. Just that you were seen leaving the home minister's office a few days ago. In fact, just two days before you called me, seeking information about a certain Shakti Pillai and his activities in Bangkok.'

'And do you have it?'

Kamat regarded Bakshi for a long moment.

'Sir, we've both been around for a long time. Long enough to know that certain games need to be played, for various reasons. That much I understand.'

Bakshi said nothing.

'I only have one request,' Kamat continued. 'If there is something I need to know about your little ... venture ... I'd like to know it from you before anyone else.'

Bakshi leaned forward.

'Let's just say that I am in a position to provide assistance to certain parties that are very interested in Shakti Pillai.'

'And if this works out?'

'If it works out, it will be beneficial for both of us. For now, you're just going to have to take my word for it. The minute I'm in a position to explain further, I will.'

Kamat nodded.

'Good enough,' he said, taking an envelope out of his shirt pocket and sliding it across the table towards Bakshi. There was a slight smile on Bakshi's lips as he removed the single piece of paper and read its contents.

'You never fail to amaze me, Kamat,' he said.

Kamat accepted the compliment with a tilt of his head. Both men picked up their glasses again.

Although he was outwardly calm, Bakshi's heart was beating fast. This was the final phase of his plan, and he needed every single piece to fall into place perfectly if he was going to pull this off.

It was while watching the news alone in his house that it had slowly come to him. As a retired IPS officer, there were very few options before him. The least desirable of all was to fade away from public memory slowly but surely. What he wanted was to come back with a bang. While most people in his position would have quietly taken a job in the private sector, he had something that they didn't: a stint with a central intelligence agency.

If handled well, such a stint could result in contacts that you could use all your life, provided you came through for them when they were in a crunch. Bakshi had realised the benefits of cultivating contacts very early in his career, and had been particularly good at it.

If there was one thing that the Indian government wanted desperately, it was Shakti Pillai. Getting him back while operating within the system was next to impossible. And operating outside the system was a challenge in itself; something only a few people, including him, could pull off. And if this worked, he thought, it would be a slap in the face of all those who had written him off, including the chief minister who had transferred him over an SMS.

'You know,' Kamat said after taking a sip of his drink. 'It's true, what they say. Things only start moving when Delhi is involved in the picture.'

Bakshi looked up at Kamat from his glass.

'What do you mean?' he said.

'This. Your little operation. The man's pretty much been wreaking hell in Mumbai for years now. But he accepts a hit on one man close to the Centre, and "certain parties" suddenly become interested in him.' Kamat chuckled.

Bakshi stared at him.

'What on earth are you talking about?'

It was Kamat's turn to stare.

'You don't know?'

'Know what?!'

Kamat stared for another moment before standing up. He went to an inner room of the cottage and came back with a thin folder.

'Got this yesterday from a Bangkok-based deep cover agent. We're still verifying it. I simply assumed that whatever you're doing was connected to it and decided to carry this report with me.'

Bakshi opened the folder and quickly skimmed through the single-page report. Then he read the report again, slowly. He read it a third time, after which he looked up.

'Kamat,' he said. 'I owe you double now.'

24

'I'VE SPOKEN TO the commissioner,' Kaewnan said as he handed out the pistols. 'We keep our distance and only step in if there is any danger to civilian life. And by civilian, I mean anyone not associated with Pillai or fucking Sangsorn.'

He handed Agarkar a gun but held on to it.

'Officially, you're not here. So, you only use this for self-defence, and stay out of sight at all times,' he said, and Agarkar nodded.

Kaewnan turned to Soseetha.

'You're on Saba Mansoor. Stay across the street from the casino. Keep an eye out for her. Go for her the minute you see her come out. Sukchai, you watch the rear. Same orders.'

Both Thai cops nodded. Kaewnan turned around and started the ignition.

The four cops had rendezvoused outside the Chong Nonski sky train station, where Sukchai had parked her car. She and Agarkar got into Kaewnan's car where he was waiting for them with Soseetha.

Soseetha had, at the beginning of their operation, arranged for eight pistols and plenty of ammunition as

Kaewnan did not want to risk losing a police issue gun and have it traced back to him or the RTP armoury. Kaewnan handed out three guns and took one for himself, and each of them got two extra clips of 9-mm ammunition.

As Kaewnan started the car and sped to the casino site, Sukchai reached out and gave Agarkar's hand a quick squeeze. He returned it and let go.

'So, after she left her hotel, she went to her warehouse and emerged twenty minutes later in disguise. She was wearing a wig—Rastafarian hair. Could pass off as a man. Got into a truck which was parked by the warehouse and drove off. We tracked her using our surveillance unit, telling them to back off whenever she passed by a CCTV camera. Fortunately, we didn't lose her,' Kaewnan told the others.

'You think she's going to hit the casino?' Agarkar asked.

'That's the only thing I can think of. In fact, that is exactly what I had been planning all along. That's why I asked Soseetha to get those explosives. Now it looks like Saba's doing the job for us. And Sangsorn is sure to blame Pillai for this.'

They drew up at the casino site, and Soseetha got off. Kaewnan drove around to the back where he dropped off Sukchai before driving back to the front. Soseetha was nowhere to be seen but that didn't worry either Kaewnan or Agarkar. His orders were to stay out of sight.

'We're trying to find Sangsorn so that we can keep an eye on him,' Kaewnan said. 'If she really does hit the casino, maybe he'll forget to take the usual precautions before contacting Pillai, and we may get a fix on his location. We've also tapped all of Shetty's phones that we know about.'

'Or maybe we'll just find the bastard Pillai's body somewhere in a day or two and we can go out and celebrate.'

Kaewnan was going to chuckle but it caught in his throat as the sound of automatic gunfire erupted inside the casino construction site.

The two cops looked at each other before springing out of the car.

✦

Venus crouched behind a row of parked cars, listening to the bullets bounce off the other side, patiently waiting for a break in the gunfire, indicating that the shooters were reloading.

She had sort of expected something like this when she had set out. When she had driven up to the gate of the site, she had a silenced gun in the seat beside her just in case the security guard got suspicious. He hadn't. He had just glanced at her, with her dreadlocks and beard and the truck, and waved her through.

She had driven under the watchful gaze of other guards at the site. During her visit with Shetty, she had recorded every detail in her mind, including the spot where the supply trucks were parked. Shetty had mentioned that the supply trucks would come in late at night so that work could start at dawn, and she had her opportunity. She liked working at night. Less traffic, less people, less collateral damage.

After the repeated hits that Pillai had taken, she had been expecting either him or Sangsorn to increase the security at the casino site. She had taken no chances. At her behest, Hammer had tipped off Sangsorn, taking care to maintain multiple layers between himself and the crime lord, that the casino was going to be attacked.

The plan was simple. A raging gun battle at a construction site was bound to attract attention from everywhere, including the media and the police. Sangsorn, if he was as smart as they said, would cut Pillai loose and wash his hands off the casino. And then, Pillai would either try to flee the country or get arrested. Venus had plans ready for either scenario. She just wanted to ensure Sangsorn was out of the picture first, because he was powerful and vindictive, and frankly, she didn't need the headache.

Driving past the corner where the supply trucks were parked, she had headed straight to the casino's grand entrance, turned around, and parked the truck with its back facing the entrance.

She then nonchalantly got out of the truck with her backpack, slung it over her shoulder, and started walking. She made it to within ten feet of the gate when someone noticed the truck and shouted out in Thai.

Turning around, she saw three men run out of the building, all of them armed with Tec-9 submachine guns. She dove behind the cars just as they started shooting and then she pulled out her MP5 submachine gun.

✦

Kaewnan and Agarkar ran through the deserted compound till they got close enough to the gunfire. Then Kaewnan pulled Agarkar behind a huge, industrial-sized dumpster. They got through the gate unhindered as the guard had run inside to investigate as soon as the first shot was heard.

'Let's wait and watch,' he whispered as the disguised woman popped out from behind the parked cars and fired three bursts.

'What about the guards?' Agarkar asked.

Kaewnan said nothing. Agarkar turned his attention to the woman. She was clearly well trained and experienced, he thought, watching her move from behind the dumpster. Next to him, Kaewnan was thinking the same thing. They saw two of the three armed men get cut down by her gun, while the third took cover behind the very truck she had parked minutes ago.

From the first floor of the building, four men were also raining bullets at her from the windows. Sangsorn was clearly taking no chances.

✦

Venus crouched behind the cars just as the first sirens were heard in the distance. This was it, she thought. She dug her hand into her jacket pocket and came up with the detonator.

More bullets pounded into the cars she was taking cover behind. She risked a quick peek and saw that five to six of the hired guards were coming closer to her.

Good, she thought. The farther away they were from the truck, the better.

The sirens were almost at the gate now. It was time. She depressed the switch on the detonator and released it.

The blast sent a massive shockwave throughout the site and out into the street. The five guards who were shooting at her fell to the ground. Unknown to her, so did Kaewnan and Agarkar.

The bomb was designed in a way that most of the damage would be sustained by anything behind the truck. In this case, it was the casino building itself. Thousands of pieces of shrapnel, along with burning embers from the truck itself, ripped through its windows and pockmarked its walls. The truck was hurled in the air and flew backwards, smashing thorough the grand entrance and coming to rest on the lobby floor, burning furiously.

Venus picked herself up, tossed the detonator aside, kicked away the backpack and started running. There was nothing in the backpack that could be traced back to her.

'Saba!' she heard a voice call out. 'Saba Mansoor! Stop!'

She turned around to see a Thai man walking towards her. He had a pistol in his hand and it was aimed right at her. There was another man behind him, also armed, also aiming at her.

'Do not move,' the man called out. 'Stay where you are.'

Venus stood still, and Kaewnan saw that she was unarmed. Confidently he walked up to her, and then she moved so fast, he didn't even realise it for two seconds. She snapped her leg upwards, connecting with his wrist, sending his gun flying. Even as Kaewnan's eyes followed his gun, Saba took one step forward and used her other leg to kick him in the solar plexus, driving him into the man behind him.

Both men fell to the ground on top of each other. Venus turned to run, but Kaewnan managed to catch hold of one of her legs. Aware that the policemen could come rushing in any minute, Venus raised her other leg and brought it down, hard, on his throat. Kaewnan's hand flew to his throat and he started thrashing around.

Turning, she saw that Agarkar was getting up. She delivered a kick to his chest, sending him back down again. She turned and ran just as the first of the cops came pouring in through the gate. The one in the lead stretched out both his arms. She tensed, preparing to attack him, but instead he started waving her away from the gate. She immediately put on her best panicked expression and ran away from the gate.

Outside, Soseetha, who had come out of his hiding place in a darkened alley after the blast, saw her crossing the street at a sprint through the chaos and drew his gun. Venus saw him and, without breaking her stride, launched herself at him. She connected with him just as he was raising his gun. As he fell, his pistol fired once, adding to the pandemonium on the street.

As he was struggling back to his feet, Venus, who was on top of him, crushed his nose with an open-palmed strike and followed it up with a chop to his neck, knocking him out.

She picked herself up and quickly slipped into an alley, pulling off her wig and leather jacket. As she emerged on the other side of the alley, she pulled out a pair of glasses and slipped them on, while also letting her hair loose. Then she started walking towards the Chong Nonski sky train station.

✦

Sukchai came running around the corner just as the first of the paramedics arrived on the scene. When she heard the explosion, her first instinct was to go running towards the sound. But her orders were to stay close to the rear exit of the casino site no matter what, so that she could watch out for Saba Mansoor.

So she stayed put, listening to the gunfire that continued after the blast, and then the sirens. It was only when Agarkar called her and told her to get inside as soon as she could that she moved from her post and ran to the casino site.

The first thing she saw was Soseetha sprawled out on the ground, bleeding from his face. She rushed over to him and checked for a pulse, after which she yelled for paramedics. As they went to work on him, she asked them which hospital they were taking him to and then crossed the street, pulling her ID around her neck as she walked through the gate.

The casino site looked like a bombed-out structure in a war-torn country. The building was totally ruined and so were many vehicles parked in the large compound. She pushed through the crowd and looked in vain for Agarkar and Kaewnan till she came to a small crowd of cops near an industrial dumpster.

Agarkar was sitting on the ground smoking a cigarette while three uniformed officers were throwing an unending barrage of questions at him in Thai. She recognised one of them and called out to him. He looked around and nodded to her.

'He's with us,' she told the officer.

'Yeah? Who's "us"?' he asked.

'Just talk to Kaewnan. He'll tell you everything,' she said as she pushed past him. 'You okay?' she asked Agarkar, kneeling in front of him and laying a hand on his shoulder. 'Where's Kaewnan?'

She looked around, hoping to find her boss, which was when she saw him. She caught a glimpse of his face just as the paramedic zipped the body bag shut over it.

Her officer friend caught her by her shoulders as she almost fell to the ground, and helped her to a sitting position.

'Crushed larynx,' Agarkar said tonelessly. 'He suffocated before help got here.'

25

'WOULD I BE calling the home minister of the country at 2.30 in the morning if it was not urgent?' Bakshi barked furiously into the phone. His tone seemed to have the desired effect, and five minutes later, he was speaking to Home Minister Prakash Sardesai.

'Is this about our meeting the other day, Ranjit?' Sardesai asked.

'It very much is, sir,' Bakshi answered. 'I have just emailed you a report. I request you to go through it and think about what we discussed.'

There was silence as Sardesai read his email.

Bakshi waited impatiently till Sardesai came back on the line.

'And you are sure of this?'

'Sir, this comes from someone I take very seriously. I wish I could tell you who, but I simply can't.'

There was another silence during which Bakshi was sure Sardesai could hear him grinding his teeth.

Finally, Sardesai spoke.

'I'll call you in ten minutes.'

'Sir ...'

'Ranjit, I am fully aware of the urgency of the situation. Now let me do what I have to do. I'll call you in ten minutes.'

✦

Narong Anantasu, commissioner of the Metropolitan Police, looked like he had aged ten years in the last one hour.

Shortly after Kaewnan's death, Sukchai had called Anantasu, and after speaking to him for ten minutes, she had handed her cell phone to Agarkar.

'Please go to my office and wait for me there,' Anantasu told him.

'I'll need to brief my commissioner, sir,' Agarkar said.

'Of course. Just get out of there before the situation gets complicated. We will talk in my office.'

Agarkar hailed a cab and went to the RTP headquarters at Rama Road, while Sukchai went with Kaewnan's body to the hospital.

Anantasu's assistant was expecting him and she showed him into a small conference room, from where Agarkar called Mathur. The top cop had already had a brief conversation with Anantasu.

'I hear things went down really bad there,' Mathur said.

'Yes, sir.'

'Tell me there's an up-side to this, Agarkar.'

'A cop is dead, sir. That works the same way here as it works there.'

Agarkar could hear Mathur sigh.

'Let me know what happens,' he said before hanging up.

Agarkar used the time to call Sultan, who was at home.

'Lie low,' he told the hitman. 'Captain Kaewnan has been killed and there's going to be a massive crackdown. I'll call you as soon as we figure out our next move.'

Half an hour later, Anantasu's assistant entered the conference room and told him that the commissioner was ready to meet him. Agarkar walked into Anantasu's office to see Anantasu and Sukchai waiting for him.

'How is Kaewnan's wife?' he asked.

'Shattered,' Anantasu said despondently. 'She doesn't even know why her husband died.'

For a minute, no one said anything. Then Anantasu stood up and walked to the window.

'He was a good man, sir,' Agarkar said. He didn't know what else to say.

Anantasu turned around, his eyes blazing.

'Mr Agarkar, that man, the man whose widow I just met, risked his life no less than five times in his career to save innocent civilians from dying. He was one of my most reliable men and one of the few good men I had left. So don't tell me he was a good man!' he said.

Agarkar looked away. Sukchai had tears in her eyes.

Anantasu slowly walked to where they were sitting and came to a stop in front of them. Agarkar stood up.

'I'm sorry, sir. I don't know what else to say.'

Anantasu said nothing.

'I'll understand if you want to put a stop to this ...'

'Do I have a choice?' Anantasu snapped.

The senior cop started pacing the room.

'Remember what I said to you the first time you came here to meet me, Mr Agarkar? I said, let us do something good together. So, now I ask you. Have we? Have we done any good?'

Sukchai stood up.

'With all due respect, sir, we have. We have done everything we can. We have delivered tremendous blows to Pillai's activities here. I know Kaewnan's dead, but so is Pillai and Sangsorn's casino.'

Anantasu glared at her.

'Kaewnan was my best friend on the force, sir. He was my best friend in this damned city. He was my anchor, my rock. And I know that he would hate me for not acknowledging the good work that we have done. So yes. We have done a lot of good together.'

Agarkar put out a hand to calm her down and she pushed it away.

'He could have just stood by, you know,' she said. 'He could have let that woman rip the casino apart and kill everyone there and walk away. But after the casino was destroyed, he went after her. You know why? Because he was a cop and she is here on a forged passport wreaking havoc with bombs and guns on our soil. He died doing his job!'

She suddenly sat down, spent.

'What do you want to do?' Anantasu asked quietly.

Before Sukchai could say anything, Agarkar spoke up.

'Avenge his death,' he said.

They both looked at him.

'Find the woman. Find Pillai. Bring in Sangsorn. Bring in Shetty. I think that bloodbath at the casino will give us enough justification to do all these things.'

Sukchai nodded.

'Shetty will have a hard time explaining why there were men with submachine guns guarding his casino site. If we squeeze him hard enough, he will give us Pillai. But we need to do all this before Pillai flees the country. He might be doing so at this very moment,' she said.

'We could even bring in Shetty's family and offer them protection in exchange for cooperation,' Agarkar added.

'We could,' Anantasu said. 'In fact, we will. But you,' he looked at Agarkar, 'and you,' he said to Sukchai, 'will not be a part of it. You're done.'

Both Agarkar and Sukchai stared at him in shocked silence.

'You go on leave till this is sorted out,' Anantasu said to Sukchai. 'And you,' he said to Agarkar, 'can catch some rest now. But I want you out of Bangkok within twenty-four hours.'

✦

Pillai, dead tired, was about to get into bed when his phone rang. He cursed.

He had just got off the phone after a lengthy call with his men, who had briefed him about the damage sustained at the casino site and the trouble it was going to bring with it. He had paced about, half expecting a hit squad from Sangsorn to barge into his house, guns blazing.

But nothing had happened for over an hour, and he had finally decided to call it a day when the call came.

It was Sangsorn.

'Listen to me carefully,' he said, sounding as if he were talking through gritted teeth. 'Against every instinct, I am refraining from killing you. Instead, a team of my trusted men will reach your place within three hours. You will go with them and they will smuggle you out of the country. I am only doing this because I want you gone. Out of my sight and out of my fucking life. Understand?'

'Th–thank you ...' Pillai began.

'Go fuck yourself, Pillai,' Sangsorn snapped. 'My people in the police force are telling me that a massive crackdown is being planned as revenge for that cop's death. Did you even know that there was a special squad working to get you? No, don't say anything. Just go with my men and disappear forever.'

'Just ... just one thing ... please?' Pillai said.

There was a pause.

'What?' Sangsorn asked finally.

'What if I make it up to you?' Pillai said.

'Do you know how much money I lost tonight, you piece of shit?'

'I'll pay you,' Pillai said. 'Tell me how much, and I'll pay you every penny.'

There was another pause.

'How?'

'I ... I have an offer, a job, back home in India. I haven't told anyone yet, not even SP. But I know I can pull it off, and the remuneration is huge. I won't come back here ever again, but I'd like to leave things on a good note.'

Pillai waited, his heart in his mouth. A job had landed in his lap very recently, a job that would take him way up there in the hierarchy of the underworld. Sangsorn would be a powerful friend to have.

'You have thirty days,' Sangsorn said.

'Done.'

Sangsorn hung up and turned to his men.

'Change of plan,' he said. 'Keep him alive.'

✦

'You remember all those hours we spent talking about how we would go?' Khanna chuckled through the blood in his mouth.

Venus wiped the blood with a handkerchief and held his hand tightly.

'All those hours of training and experience. Remember how we talked about how we would finally meet our end? You said something about growing old and dying alone in a mansion.' Khanna chuckled again.

'Stop talking,' she said.

They had barely made it to the safe house after the confrontation with the drug dealers holed up in Antwerp. The job was a simple snatch and grab. The seven men had received payment for a massive shipment of drugs in the form of a case full of uncut diamonds worth billions of dollars, and their client was very interested in it. They were being paid 20 per cent of the diamonds' worth, and had already received half of it in advance.

'What did I tell you?' he asked her.

'Sir … stop …' she said, fighting back the tears.

The job had seemed simple enough, till they slipped into the drug dealers' hideout and found them awake and within reaching distance of AK-56 assault rifles, instead of being stoned out of their minds in the wake of their big deal. They weren't celebrating, as Venus and Khanna had been informed. They had been tipped off and were on high alert. They were waiting in the darkened cottage, ready for the attack.

The quiet neighbourhood was awoken to the booming sounds of automatic gunfire as a full-scale gun battle started inside the cottage. The minute they slipped inside the cottage through the windows, the drug dealers flipped on the lights and raised their automatic rifles. Both Khanna and Venus went into autopilot, operating on sheer instinct, ducking, shooting, rolling, leaping, simultaneously focusing on killing and not being killed.

'What did I tell you?' Khanna repeated.

'A lucky shot,' Venus whispered.

It wasn't even a direct hit. A round from one of the drug dealer's assault rifles ricocheted off the stone wall of the cottage and pierced his neck. The next instant, Venus rolled up behind the shooter and put a bullet in his head. He was the last one and Venus managed to drag a heavily bleeding Khanna to their van and sped away just as the sirens were heard in the distance.

Now she sat in their safe house, cradling his head in her lap; he was pale from the loss of blood.

'I've seen it ... so ... many times,' Khanna said. 'In the army, after that ... so many of my friends ... One lucky hit ... and it's over ...'

'Sir ...' she said.

At that instant, Khanna's hand went limp in hers.

The memory, after all these years, was still fresh in her mind. She had never forgotten the feeling of his hand going limp. She too had been a hardened veteran by then, no longer in need of a mentor to protect her. But it had still felt like something inside her had quietly died. He had been the only person she cared for in the world. And he was gone.

He had been right. People like her and Khanna spent hours practising to ensure that all weak spots were covered, all the time. They took care to stay behind cover to prevent being shot by snipers, even while doing something as simple as walking down a street. When they got into a firefight, they always identified the best possible spot to take cover. In hand-to-hand combat, they always made sure not to take a blow to the vulnerable parts.

And it was always one lucky hit from someone who probably didn't even realise it, that finally brought them down.

The pain was increasing and she was starting to feel dizzy.

She first realised it after she hailed a cab from near the Chong Nonski sky train station to go to her hotel in Thonburi. As the adrenaline wore off, she became aware of a dull pain in her side. She touched it and her hand came away covered in blood. She slouched back in her seat and smiled.

The heavily built policeman she had tackled at the mouth of the alley must have no idea how lucky he was. He had managed to get off a single shot as she leaped at him, and the pistol round had gone through her left side. She was bleeding out.

There was only one thing left to do. She pulled out her cell phone from her pocket and started typing. It took her a good two minutes to finish the task.

26

'YOU'RE SURE ABOUT THIS?' Agarkar asked, checking the ammunition clip in his pistol.

Sukchai said nothing as she focused on the road in front of her and steadily depressed the accelerator.

After leaving Anantasu's office, Sukchai and Agarkar had parted ways at the parking lot. Agarkar had left for the warehouse that had served as their headquarters for over two weeks, while Sukchai had gone to the King Chulalongkorn Memorial Hospital to check on Soseetha.

'I'll see you at the warehouse,' she had told Agarkar as they hugged before leaving.

She reached the warehouse an hour later, aware of a feeling of extreme exhaustion. Doctors at the hospital had told her that apart from a broken nose, which had been fixed, and a couple of bruises, there was nothing wrong with Soseetha, and that he would be out in a day or two.

Agarkar was sprawled out on one of the cots in one corner of the warehouse, fast asleep. She went to the bathroom and took a hot shower, after which she changed into the spare clothes she kept in the warehouse. Going back to the cots, she snuggled in beside Agarkar, who was so tired that he didn't even twitch.

She was drifting into a tired slumber when she became aware of an insistent buzzing somewhere in the deep recesses of her consciousness. She fought off the exhaustion and focused on the sound. It took her a second to realise that her cell phone was buzzing.

She reached out and picked it up. It was the IT expert whose help she had sought to track down the IP address which was suspected to have been used by Pillai.

'That IP address you gave me,' he rasped into the phone, 'is it connected to Kaewnan's death?'

The expert had been a good friend of hers as well as Kaewnan's and he had helped them innumerable times in the past. Like Kaewnan, he was simply interested in doing some good.

'Yes,' Sukchai replied, sitting up. 'Yes, it is.'

'The IP just got active,' the man on the other end said. 'I'm sending you the location.'

Sukchai's breath caught in her throat.

'Th … thank you,' she managed.

He told her that the IP address had exchanged data with another in Rangsit, which turned out to be Raghav Shetty's address.

'I hope you kill the bastard,' the IT expert said before hanging up.

Five minutes later, she was shaking Agarkar awake. Fifteen minutes later, they were running to Sukchai's car, which was parked outside.

Now, as they sped towards the address in the upmarket Samut Prakarn, Agarkar repeated, 'Are you sure about this?'

'Stop asking me that,' she said through gritted teeth.

'Damn it, Sukchai. Anantasu made himself clear.'

'I don't care.'

'You could lose your job over this.'

'Pretty sure I'm going to. But after this, it won't matter.'

They picked up Sultan on the way.

'We're already in enough shit, so do exactly as you're told,' Agarkar told Sultan, who nodded.

It was just past dawn and traffic on the roads wasn't too heavy, which was why they made the two-and-a-half-hour drive in just under two hours.

Around the corner from the villa where the IP address was located, Sultan got out of the car.

'Stay close and stay alert. I need someone out here in case he manages to run,' Agarkar told Sultan, who cocked his weapon, slid it into his waistband, and nodded.

After checking their pistols one last time, Sukchai and Agarkar looked at each other and nodded. Sukchai started the ignition and stepped on the accelerator.

Agarkar looked out of his window and scanned the houses on his side, checking for any lookouts that Pillai might have posted in the neighbourhood.

'Whatever happens today, I want you to know one thing,' Agarkar said, without looking at Sukchai.

She said nothing and he turned to look at her. Immediately, he knew something was wrong. Sukchai was staring dead ahead with a strange expression on her face, and he realised that the car was slowing down as well.

Agarkar followed her gaze and froze. He counted five police cars parked outside a villa around a hundred metres away, and the approach had been barricaded. Several policemen, uniformed as well as in plainclothes, were milling about.

'What the fuck?' he said.

'Wait for me,' Sukchai said, pulling to a halt and unfastening her seat belt.

As she stepped out of the car, Agarkar dialled Sultan's number.

'Get out,' he told Sultan. 'Wait for us at the warehouse.'

Sukchai took a good fifteen minutes to return. She mutely got into the driver's seat, turned the car around and started driving.

'Well?' Agarkar asked. 'Who were those guys and what were they doing there?'

'Crime Investigation Bureau,' she answered. 'Pillai was picked up half an hour ago. The commissioner general has granted approval for his extradition to India and the diplomatic process starts tomorrow.'

✦

Three Days Ago ...

SP was hurting all over. When he had opened his eyes, a nurse had told him that he had been unconscious for over a day, and that he had been lucky to survive his fall.

SP said nothing.

On the night that Sangsorn had summoned Pillai, he had been waiting in the car when one of Sangsorn's bouncers had told him that he was needed inside. SP had followed the bouncer into the nightclub and into a private room, where three others were waiting for him.

He didn't remember much after that.

Six hours after he woke up, an Indian man walked into his room, smiling at him.

'Who are you?' SP asked bluntly. The painkillers were wearing off and he was getting irritable.

The man pulled out a cell phone, made a call and waited for a minute before handing the phone to him.

'Who are you?' SP repeated.

The man said nothing. SP refused to move.

'I'm just going to stand here, you know,' the man said.

SP reluctantly took the cell phone and put it to his ear.

'*Kaisa hai*, SP?' the familiar voice on the other end said, and SP felt a shiver go down his spine.

'B-Bakshi sahab?' he asked, shocked.

'Good to hear your voice too,' Bakshi said from his hotel room in Kodaikanal.

'How did you find me?'

'Not important, SP. Not important. Just listen,' Bakshi said.

There were a few short mechanical sounds, after which a recording started playing.

'*What, Kulkarni sahab, are you very angry?*' The first voice was definitely Shakti Pillai's.

'*Stop the joking, Pillai. What are you up to?*' It took a moment for SP to recognise the voice of Joint Commissioner Satish Kulkarni, Mumbai Crime Branch.

'*What will you do now, sir? I had to send out a message. That bastard Alam has been hitting out at me. I can't just be taking it sitting down, right?*'

'*Oh, shut up! A shootout in the middle of a residential area? And then your idiots start a fire in the building?*'

'*You are right to be angry, sir.*'

'*I'm not looking for your fucking approval, Pillai. I'm going to be hurting you, badly.*'

'*How about I make it easier for you?*'

'*What the fuck do you mean?*'

'*SP is currently admitted to the Bangkok Christian Hospital. He's not going anywhere for a couple of weeks at least. Doctors said he has broken ribs and has suffered head injuries.*'

There was silence for a moment.

'*Are you suggesting ...?*' Kulkarni finally said.

'*He's all yours, Kulkarni sahab. Pick him up and take him away. You can have a nice press conference after you take him to India.*'

After another moment's silence, Kulkarni said, '*Which hospital, did you say?*'

Bakshi stopped the recording and came back on the line.

'Want to hear more?' he asked.

'Why should I believe you?' SP countered.

'Because, irrespective of what you might think, my target is your boss, not you.'

'What are you saying?'

'I'm saying you get me your boss and I'll make sure Kulkarni doesn't touch you. And trust me, I can make that happen.'

'And I am just supposed to take your word for that?'

'Look, it's either that or you come back to India, after which you spend the rest of your life inside a cell. That, I can definitely make sure of.'

SP said nothing.

'One more thing. Get in touch with your people and ask them about the latest contract that your boss has accepted.'

'What are you talking about?' SP snapped.

'I'm sure you'll find out in no time,' Bakshi said before hanging up.

SP moved the phone away from his ear and stared at it for a beat before handing it over to the man, who was now sitting in a chair near his bed.

'Keep it,' the man said. 'Get well soon.'

SP spent the next hour making calls using his own cell phone, finding out what was happening in the gang while he was chained to the bed. He could not believe what he was hearing.

The day Pillai's men had attacked Wajid Qureshi's house in Dongri, Pillai had apparently got a call from someone in India. This man had offered Pillai ten crore rupees in exchange for an attack on an MLA in the ruling party.

Pillai had already found out that the MLA had moved to a government bungalow opposite the Mantralaya after winning the election, and that he stepped out for a walk after dinner on most nights. Pillai was readying shooters who could do a drive-by shooting and speed away on motorcycles on Marine Drive, which was a minute's distance from the MLA's bungalow.

SP gritted his teeth furiously. The reckless idiot was going to take everyone down with him.

He reached under his pillow and grabbed the cell phone that Bakshi's man had left with him.

✦

Mathur was in his office when his phone rang. He picked it up and straightened in his seat on being told that it was Union Home Minister Sardesai who was on the line.

'Yes, sir,' Mathur said.

'Mathur, I have some news for you. Shakti Pillai was picked up in Bangkok a short while ago.'

'I heard, sir. I was just about to call your office to find out whose operation it was.'

Mathur had actually received a call from Agarkar half an hour ago.

'It was my operation, Mathur. Central agencies were running it under my supervision,' Sardesai said condescendingly. He had never liked Mathur.

'I see, sir.'

'I want you to send a team to Bangkok with Pillai's dossier and fingerprints. I have spoken to their government and these are all just formalities.'

'Right, sir.'

'Good. Keep me posted.'

'Yes, sir. Oh, there's another thing, sir, which I thought I should let you know.'

There was a pause.

'Yes, Mathur?'

'There's been another development in Bangkok, coincidentally …' Mathur began.

27

It was late afternoon, the day after Pillai's arrest, when Sukchai brought her car to a halt in the parking lot of the King Chulalongkorn Memorial Hospital.

For a while, she just sat in her seat, her hands on the wheel, till Agarkar spoke to her from the passenger seat.

'What are you thinking?'

She turned to him.

'This is goodbye, isn't it?' she asked.

Agarkar was booked on a flight to India in three hours and would go to the airport directly after leaving the hospital.

Saying nothing, he reached out and put one hand on hers. She drew closer and they pulled each other into a tight hug, neither of them wanting to let go.

'Remember what I was saying when we were driving to Pillai's location?' he said softly, his face buried in her shoulder.

'You got as far as "whatever happens today I want you to know one thing" before—'

'Before it all went to hell.' He chuckled. 'Yeah. I just want you to know that Kaewnan would be proud of you.'

Sukchai stifled a sob.

'I mean it,' Agarkar said, stroking her hair. 'And you should know that my commissioner will be writing a long letter of recommendation to Anantasu.'

Sukchai broke the embrace and looked at him.

'Funny you should say that,' she said. 'Anantasu texted me half an hour ago saying he's just finished writing something similar for you.'

Agarkar smiled.

'Wow,' he said softly.

They kissed tenderly for a long time before pulling away from each other.

'Let's go see the big man,' Agarkar said.

Soseetha had recovered enough to be discharged and they had come to pick him up so that Agarkar could say goodbye before leaving.

Perhaps for the first time since Agarkar had met him, Soseetha was not smiling. The previous day, just after Sukchai and Agarkar had returned to the warehouse in Suan Luang, Soseetha had called to ask about Kaewnan.

'I can't reach boss's phone. Is he okay?' he had asked.

Sukchai had gently broken the news to him, adding that he had died at the hands of the woman they knew as Saba Mansoor.

'Any word on the woman?' Soseetha asked the instant he saw Sukchai and Agarkar walk into his room.

Agarkar went over to Soseetha's bed and laid a hand on his shoulder.

'We heard this morning. After the shootout, she hailed a cab to the hotel in Thonburi where she was staying. This was after her run-in with you,' Agarkar said.

Soseetha scowled at the memory.

'However, she got out of the cab midway. The driver noticed that she was bleeding, but she waved a gun in his face and sent him packing.'

'And ...?'

'The details of what happened next are sketchy, but this morning, the police pulled a badly mangled car out of the Chao Phraya river, with the body still inside. The face was damaged badly, but the autopsy confirmed a bullet wound to the left, just like the cab driver had described, and the clothes were the same as those we saw on Saba. The car was stolen last night. Cause of death was drowning.'

Soseetha's face changed.

'You got her, big man.' Agarkar smiled at him.

Soseetha looked as if he was going to cry. Agarkar squeezed his shoulder and Sukchai took his hand in hers.

'What about the mission?' Soseetha asked, pulling himself together. Taking turns, Sukchai and Agarkar brought him up to date on the developments of the last twelve hours while he listened in wonder.

'Wow!' he said finally. 'And this man, Bakshi, he was in on it all along?'

'The official story is that the home minister brought him in as a consultant due to his knowledge of and experience with the Mumbai underworld.'

'He's that good, huh?' Soseetha asked.

'If there's one man more devious than Mathur, it has to be him.'

'And that's not all,' Sukchai told him. 'Apparently, Pillai had accepted a contract on a senior politician in India. The Indian government finally lost its patience with him and our government agreed, and now he's on his way back.'

'Speaking of losing patience ...' Agarkar said, smiling. 'Tell him about Sangsorn.'

'What about Sangsorn?' Soseetha asked.

'Well, looks like the commissioner general lost patience with the commander after that bloodbath at the casino, and the commander lost patience with Sangsorn. We pulled in Shetty and asked him to explain why there were men armed with unlicensed submachine guns at his construction site or go to jail for a really long time. It was Agarkar's idea.'

Agarkar grinned modestly.

'We also picked up his entire family and the commander offered a foolproof protection plan, including safe passage to whatever country he wanted to move to,' he said.

'Shetty cooperated?' Soseetha asked, wide-eyed.

'With Pillai gone, he didn't have any reason not to. He spilled the beans on the entire unholy nexus and, as we speak, he's being put on a private jet to a destination which he will only reveal to the pilot after they are airborne. CIB teams are raiding Sangsorn's spots across Bangkok right now,' Sukchai finished.

Soseetha gave a little whoop and pulled both of them into a hug.

'Okay, okay, big man,' Agarkar said, patting his back. 'Let's go see about getting you out of here.'

'We brought you a change of clothes,' Sukchai said, handing him the bag she was carrying.

They walked to the door and were holding hands as soon as they were out in the corridor. Agarkar pulled her close to him.

Looking up at him, Sukchai kissed him on the lips and he returned the kiss. Then they just stood in the corridor holding each other for another minute before letting go. They both thought of something to say, and they both realised it was not necessary, so they simply turned and walked together to the nurses' station.

The formalities were completed in fifteen minutes and Soseetha was dressed and asking the nurse about removing the bandage from his broken nose when they walked in. The nurse complained to Sukchai in Thai, telling her to get Soseetha to leave the bandage alone, and Sukchai laughed before assuring her that she would.

'Hey,' Soseetha said. 'What happened to SP?'

Sukchai frowned.

'He's disappeared,' she said.

Agarkar grinned.

'Oh yeah. I forgot to tell you. It was SP who helped Bakshi find Pillai. Bakshi's made him disappear.'

Sukchai stared at him.

'How long have you known?' she demanded.

'Just before we left for the hospital,' Agarkar said, raising his hands defensively. 'I swear I simply forgot.'

'Also,' Soseetha intervened, 'what about Sultan?'

Agarkar and Sukchai looked at each other and smiled.

28

'... THE DECEASED, SULTAN AZIZ, is said to have been one of the most loyal hitmen for underworld don Maqsood Alam, and has no less than thirteen murder cases registered against him in Mumbai from the early '90s, when Alam was still in Mumbai. Aziz was among the few trusted aides that Alam took with him when he fled the country in the late '90s. Alam is now believed to be in Dubai.'

Bakshi watched with amusement as the television channel flashed file photos of Aziz in succession while the newscaster's voice continued in the background.

There was a discreet knock on the door and Bakshi looked up to see Mathur standing in the doorway. Bakshi waved him in, returning his attention to the TV screen.

'Sources in the Metropolitan Police tell us that Aziz was staying in Bangkok under the name Ayaaz Ali, using a passport which is believed to have been obtained from Pakistan using forged documents. Aziz was reportedly in Bangkok on a job to settle a score in the bitter rivalry between Maqsood Alam and Shakti

Pillai. Coincidentally, Pillai was arrested in Bangkok by the CIB of the RTP on the same day as Aziz was shot dead by Lieutenant Arunee Sukchai of the RTP.'

'Do sit, Mathur,' Bakshi said, still watching the news report.

'Aziz is being linked to a shootout and a blast that occurred at the site of a casino in Silom, which left five men dead and property worth millions of baht damaged. The owner of the casino site, an Indian national named Raghav Shetty, is believed to have had links with Pillai, which reportedly led to the attack.'

Bakshi chuckled.

'The incident at the casino site also left Captain Anurak Kaewnan dead and Lieutenant Sitthichok Soseetha injured, and the latter is now out of danger. Narong Anantasu, commander of the Metropolitan Police, has gone on record saying that the investigation against Aziz benefited to a large degree with the help of Inspector Dayanand Agarkar of the Mumbai Police. Currently posted with the Andheri Police Station, Mr Agarkar, a former Crime Branch officer with a reputation of being an "encounter specialist", was sent by Mumbai Police Commissioner Satish Mathur to assist the Metropolitan Police, after Mr Agarkar received a tip-off about Aziz being in Bangkok.'

Bakshi turned to Mathur.

'Quite noble, Mathur,' he said. 'Letting Agarkar claim the credit. You could have easily claimed that it was your tip-off.'

'I am told that sharing credit with one's subordinates takes one a long way, sir,' Mathur said, smiling thinly, and Bakshi chuckled again.

'The operation to arrest Pillai was a top secret one supervised by Union Home Minister Prakash Sardesai. It was revealed only two days ago that retired DGP Ranjit Bakshi was part of the operation on direct orders from Mr Sardesai. Mr Bakshi, apart from having served as Mumbai police commissioner, has also served with the IB for over ten years and represented India in global anti-terror conferences ...' the reporter was saying as Bakshi hit the mute button and turned to look at his junior.

Mathur was known for ensuring that the spotlight stayed with him, while making a cursory mention of his juniors, who actually did all the work.

Bakshi, on the other hand, had been, and continued to be, hugely popular among the rank and file for his tendency to acknowledge the efforts of his men. He would even mention full names of constables during live press conferences and point at them so that they got their share of the limelight. The habit, like most of his professional habits, had been carefully cultivated and had paid dividends. Every policeman who had worked with Bakshi swore by his name and was prepared to do anything for him, even after his retirement.

It was through one such policeman, now with the Crime Branch, that Bakshi had got the number that Kulkarni had used to contact Pillai. His next step had been to contact a friend in the IB, with whom he had worked during his ten-year stint with the agency, who had the power to put cell phones under surveillance.

'Want to tap a phone for me?' Bakshi had asked the man.

'No,' was the surly answer.

It had taken fifteen minutes and a lot of promises to convince the friend, but he had finally agreed.

Bakshi's study of his legendary diaries that night had established that even though SP was believed to be a loyal second-in-command, he wasn't exactly Pillai's best friend. SP had fled to Bangkok with Pillai in a moment of indecision, which he had been regretting ever since. After going to Bangkok, he had found himself stuck and all his efforts to put as much distance between the gang and the illegal operations in Bangkok were only him looking out for himself. Plus, it was a known fact that Pillai was egoistic enough to believe that he could run the gang without SP.

Bakshi had decided that SP was the weak link that could be exploited.

His next step had been his most dangerous one. Using an internet call and a voice-disguising software, Bakshi had called Pillai on one of his numbers known to the RAW but not the Mumbai Police. He knew that RAW would not share the number with the city police so that it could keep its own sources of information intact and get the occasional one up over the police.

He had not actually expected Pillai to agree to the 'supari' killing of an MLA with a ruling party, but the successful murder of the IAS officer in Bandra and the attack in Dongri had convinced Pillai that there was nothing he would not do.

'Tell me your plan and I'll send you half the money right away. I'll call in two days,' Bakshi had told Pillai and the man had taken the bait.

The same night, Bakshi's friend in the IB had emailed him an audio file with a line saying, 'Next time you get me to tap an IPS officer's phone, fucking let me know.' Bakshi had smiled sheepishly and deleted the email after downloading the voice note.

Then came the meeting with Kamat in Kodaikanal, where Kamat had given him the contact details of his man in Bangkok, who Bakshi used to contact SP. As Bakshi had expected, word of the supposed hit on the MLA had already reached RAW and they were verifying it before passing it on to the relevant authorities. Bakshi, being Kamat's friend, got a sneak preview and it was enough to spur Sardesai into action.

Across the table from him, Mathur stared at him expressionlessly.

'Why am I here, sir?' Mathur asked bluntly.

'Oh, I thought I'd congratulate you,' Bakshi said, smiling.

'You called me all the way from Mumbai to Delhi to congratulate me?'

'Among other things,' said Bakshi, opening a drawer and taking out a folder. 'Tell me,' he went on. 'Your brother was with the Delhi Police, right?'

Mathur forced himself to remain calm. Bakshi would never find out something like this without some venal motive.

'Elder brother, sir. Retired last year. He opted for the Delhi cadre after clearing his IPS. Wanted to work close to home,' Mathur replied stiffly.

'Letting you pursue your dreams of locking horns with the Mumbai underworld,' Bakshi said, smiling. 'One of his postings was in Hauz Khas, right?'

Mathur nodded. 'He was a DCP there.'

Bakshi slid the folder in his hands across the table. 'This might interest him, then.'

Mathur opened the file and his heart skipped a beat. The Hauz Khas double murder case over sixteen years ago. A couple found bludgeoned to death in their garage; teenage daughter abducted, dramatically freed herself and went missing a week later.

Mathur looked up.

'What is this?' he asked sharply.

'Turn the page, Mathur,' Bakshi said.

Mathur obeyed and saw a blow-up of a passport picture. The passport belonged to Noori Siddiqui. The daughter of Dr Asgar Siddiqui and his wife, Asira.

For years together, Mathur's elder brother had talked about nothing else. Three of the suspects had been found burned alive in a shack on the highway. The fourth had died in the hospital five days after being attacked by Noori. Mathur's brother had later learned that it was Noori's Urdu teacher who had given them the security code, and that she was killed in a hotel in Bangkok the same year. Noori, however, was never seen again.

'I wish I could find the girl, Sanjay. I wish I could just find her some day and tell her I tried to find the people responsible for her becoming an orphan,' Mathur's brother would tell him after one drink too many. The case, the goriness of it, and the girl's tormented face, had never stopped haunting him.

'Keep reading,' Bakshi said.

Mathur turned the page to see the picture of another passport, this one in the name of Saba Mansoor. Mathur straightened in his seat. It was the same name that Agarkar had told him. Mathur compared the photographs several times before he could believe it. Saba Mansoor was Noori Siddiqui.

'There's more,' Bakshi said. 'This morning, a hundred crore rupees was transferred from an untraceable account into the account of the policeman killed in Bangkok. Agarkar can easily confirm this. Another hundred crore was donated to the RTP. Plus, a hundred crore was donated to the Delhi Police.'

Mathur did not know what to say.

'And then there's this,' Bakshi finished, sliding another page across the table.

It was a printout of an email. Mathur started reading.

'I have attached all my research into the activities of Shakti Pillai with this email. This includes some indications of policemen, both Indian and Thai, who I believe are connected to him. As I understand, extradition proceedings hinge largely on evidence and I hope this helps.

You might also want to look into an illegal brothel run in Gurgaon by one Mohit Rai. This is the same brothel in which the daughter of Dr Asgar and Asira Siddiqui was to be sold after being kidnapped. Shakti Pillai is heavily involved in this brothel, and in trafficking girls as young as thirteen years old from Mumbai and Gujarat. This information has been gleaned from someone I have personally interrogated. The brothel also has connections to some loan sharks who operate in Gurgaon and Delhi. Selling young girls from their debtors' families into this brothel is one of their ways of recovering their money.

I have turned over everything I have found out, not only during my time in Bangkok, but over the last sixteen years, to the authorities, because I want to help prevent another Noori Siddiqui from being kidnapped. This is also why I am donating what I feel is a significant amount to the Delhi Police, so that it can be used to strengthen their infrastructure. Please spend it as you see fit.'

Mathur looked up in wonder.

'Sounds like a parting note, doesn't it?' Bakshi asked. 'According to what I know so far, she was found dead a couple of days later.'

Mathur nodded but didn't say anything.

'I was thinking we could put your brother on the committee that disperses the funds. I think he'd like that,' Bakshi said.

Bakshi's smile seemed to be genuine, and for a minute Mathur wondered if there was a human element still alive inside the man.

Then he thought, *Of course. Now I owe him. The bastard.*

'Thank you, sir,' he said.

'You're welcome, Mathur. You can keep that folder. Those are copies.'

Mathur stood up, picking up the folder. He was at the door when Bakshi called out his name again.

'The next time you plan a secret operation, I'd like to be kept in the loop.'

Bakshi paused.

'Even if you don't tell me, I'll find out anyway. I am no longer a retiree without access to the system.'

Mathur stared at Bakshi, but said nothing.

'You can leave,' Bakshi said, turning his swivel chair back to the TV set.

As he exited Bakshi's office, Mathur turned around to throw one last look of contempt at the freshly installed name plate over the door.

Ranjit Bakshi. IPS. National Security Advisor.

Epilogue

SHE OPENED HER eyes and for the first time her face didn't hurt.

It had been thirty days since the surgery. The doctors at the private facility in Sweden, where she had spent the past month, said that she was healing nicely.

Getting out of the bed, she went to the mirror to examine herself. She missed the cheekbones the most. They had been like her mother's. But the surgery had changed the shape of her cheekbones. They were no longer as sharp and pronounced.

She walked back slowly to her bed. Hammer had done a great job of planting the body from the morgue for the Thai Police to find. From the money she had remaining from the Pillai hit, she had wired a hundred crore rupees to Hammer for all his help, which was over and above the usual fee he charged for his assistance on her jobs.

The rest of the money she wired back to Mehra, with a promise that more would follow. He had told her that there was no need, as Pillai was out of action and he was sure she had a part to play in it.

In the cab, while she was bleeding from the bullet wound, she had realised that it was the perfect time to give up her old identity. She had been too exposed on this job, and with the kind of attention that the situation was going to attract, she was sure to be identified. It was, finally, time to get a new identity.

After getting out of the cab, the first call she had made was to Hammer, who sped to her location, gave her a shot of adrenaline and a painkiller, and rushed her to a doctor he used in such situations. Then he took care of the rest, while she emailed all her research to the Indian government.

She had first heard of Pillai around five years ago, when she returned to India and started gathering intel on the brothel she was going to be sent to after she was kidnapped. She found out it was run by Mohit Rai and learned about Pillai's association with it. Over five years, she built up a detailed dossier on the entire operation, but before she could strike, the Shakti Pillai contract had come her way. His association with Roy was the real reason she took the job.

'Ma'am?' the voice made her turn towards the door.

The young man was a low-level employee at the facility.

'This was delivered for you,' he said, entering her room and handing her a large envelope. She smiled and thanked him.

She waited for him to leave before locking the door from the inside. Then she tore open the envelope and poured its contents on the bed. As she ran her eye over them, she smiled.

New passport, new driving licence, dossier with new fictional life story. She looked at the name on the passport. Madhumita Sen. She was going to have to learn Bengali.

She gathered the fake IDs and slid them back into the envelope. Then she settled down on the bed to read her made-up life story. Time was scarce. She had already put the word out. Venus would be back in the market in three months.

Acknowledgements

PICKING THE BRAINS of police officers to look for story ideas can be a fun experience, be it a 'story' in the journalistic sense or an idea for a novel. *Assassins* was conceived way back when two gangsters were still at large and both were major irritants for the Mumbai Police. One of them was Rajendra Nikhalje, alias Chhota Rajan, and the other was Ravi Pujari.

Shakti Pillai is a mix of both of them. He has Rajan's brains and the arrogance of Pujari, who thought he could be someone to reckon with, while in reality he was just another wannabe who tried in vain to make a mark. There are recordings of his calls, where he can be heard trying to extort money from a man who ran a small fleet of water tankers.

The book began as an idle thought. What if there were some way to squash bugs like Rajan and Pillai and get them out of the way for good? It took quite some time to develop the idea, particularly because, as fantastic as it was, it needed to have some measure of realism in it. I set about bouncing the idea off some of my closest confidantes in the force, and thus several other ideas took root. One was that if the police could try to finish off a gangster on foreign soil, so could the gangster's rivals. In fact, it would be a much easier proposition for them. The idea of more than one hunter stalking a common prey appealed to me immediately.

At the same time, we also discussed inter-departmental politics and the way politicians treat senior IPS officers, and I don't exactly remember when, but somewhere down the line, I decided that it would be a disgraced IPS officer who would ultimately win the day.

There are countless stories in and around the police department that go untold for umpteen number of reasons, and if such stories can find some kind of expression through my books, I will feel I have given them their due.